35027799

PUTTING THE SHOW IN CHOIR

THE ULTIMATE HANDBOOK FOR YOUR REHEARSAL AND PERFORMANCE

BY VALERIE LIPPOLDT MACK

W9-BLF-029

To Greg Gilpin—once more, thanks for believing in me.

To my children, Stevie and Zane—thanks for reminding me of the importance of having dreams.

To my incredible husband, Tom—thanks for partnering with me and keeping my dance card full!

Thank you to all my incredibly wise mentors who have taught me so much

(Nancy, Larry, Joel, Matt, Dulcie, Anissa, Kristina, Mason, Dad, and Mom)

and for the green skies and silver box blessings!!

ISBN 978-1-61774-323-8

Shawnee Press

Exclusively Distributed By

HAL•LEONARD®
CORPORATION

7777 W. BLUEMOUND RD. P.O. BOX 13819 MILWAUKEE, WI 53213

Copyright © 2011 by HAL LEONARD CORPORATION
International Copyright Secured   All Rights Reserved
Copying is illegal

www.shawneepress.com
www.halleonard.com

ACT I

INTERMISSION

ACT II

CHAPTER 6: **ON WITH THE SHOW**

CHAPTER 7: **FROM THE LAND OF "BLAHS" TO THE LAND OF "AHS!"**

CHAPTER 8: **BEHIND THE SCENES**

CHAPTER 9: **TAKE A BOW**

PROGRAM NOTES

WHO COULD ASK FOR ANYTHING MORE?!?!?

OVERTURE...

The process of putting the "show" in choir is a most rewarding and exciting journey for any choral director. As thrilling as the excursion may be, the road can be filled with unexpected bends, twists, and turns. The process is a daunting task for the director with little experience; but with guidance it can be a fulfilling—and even life-changing—adventure for all involved. The size of the learning curve and the amount of "show" added will vary with each ensemble and season.

Music curriculums are facing budget and program cuts. If we are to recruit students, rebuild fine arts programs, and restore music in our schools, artists must set aside petty differences and learn to work together. It is our responsibility as educators to provide more than one musical approach and to present a multitude of styles for our students and audience members.

Many colleges and universities shy away from show choir class offerings and/or pop ensembles for the music education major. First-year directors must often rely on their middle school/high school experiences and memories. Show choir is a growing and changing art form. Thanks to the high-tech world and our *Idol-* and *Glee*-obsessed media, this art form will only find more attention and rapid transformation. Having spent forty years in the show choir genre, I'm offering my humble opinions about show choir topics that generate lots of inquiries. If you haven't yet ventured into this world, this handbook will give you the answers and maybe even raise a few questions.

Simply stated, choreography, when used tastefully, can complement and enhance the educational and entertainment value of the music. Motion attracts attention. But continuous motion is just as boring as no motion at all. And, of course, any movement that detracts from the vocal line or choral sound should be avoided. There must be a balance—but exactly how do we find that balance and get started? As an experienced music and dance educator, I'd like to share a few things I've learned over the years.

I grew up as the daughter of music educators. Some of my favorite childhood memories are of master clinicians who visited our home in northwest Kansas. As my parents drove to and from the nearest airport—a mere four hours away by car—I would sit in the backseat and soak up the stories and anecdotes from these larger-than-life musicians. Hearing tales from Albert McNeil, Jester Hairston, Fred Waring, Eph Ehly, Kirby Shaw, and Doug Anderson was literally life-changing. Those stories shaped my life and made me the teacher and person I am today.

I've been blessed with amazing friends and colleagues. If you see yourself in any part of the book, know that your lessons have and continue to make an impact on a bigger audience and stage. Outstanding choral performances are a perfect combination of vocals, staging, and heart—don't shortchange any of the three. The stage is set. On with the show!

~ Valerie Lippoldt Mack

BUTLER
SHOW
CHOIR
SHOW
CASE
★★★

ACT I

CHAPTER 1:
STAGE ONE

THERE'S NO BUSINESS LIKE ... MUSIC EDUCATION

Yes, I believe it is safe to say that show choirs are here to stay. In fact, thanks to shows such as *American Idol*, *America's Got Talent*, *Glee*, and *So You Think You Can Dance* (*SYTYCD*), this phenomenon may be the fastest-growing type of musical ensemble in music history. However, I firmly believe that programs must be balanced. A healthy choral program offers a variety of musical styles—all taught and performed at the highest level. Show choirs (swing choirs, jazz ensembles, music theater ensembles, etc.) should be used to attract students to the music program. The students should then get the opportunity to sing classical and traditional literature as well as the popular and show choir literature. It is imperative to incorporate all styles of music—not only for the students but also for the audience members. Students and audiences need a well-balanced diet. A diet of all cotton candy is not a good thing, but neither is a diet of strictly steak and lobster. Too much of anything may sound fun, but you will have cravings before long. Even fad diets lose their appeal after a while.

> Show choirs are here to stay

> It is imperative to incorporate all styles of music—not only for the students but also for the audience members.

SHOW CHOIR 101—EDUCATING THE DIRECTOR(S)

If you are thinking about starting a show choir or swing choir, be sure to be well-versed on show choir lingo. These phrases and definitions might come in handy.

- **Show choir (or Showchoir):** A type of singing group that performs popular or Broadway literature. The dancing is choreographed to fit everyone's style; singers wear matching and glitzy costumes; singers often pair into couples; risers and other types of levels are used; a large combo accompanies performances.

- **Swing choir**: A choir that "swings." A mix of a jazz choir and a show choir, it uses a rhythm combo that is typically smaller than a show choir combo. It employs mostly straight lines and few formations, and it rarely uses risers and levels.

- **Jazz choir**: A small jazz ensemble, normally using individual mics and improvised movements such as snaps and small arm gestures. Uses a rhythm section. The ensemble performs jazz charts and standards.

- **Show choir choreography**: Energetic staging and movement. Many groups use a hip-hop flair as most students aren't classically trained dancers. The choreography depends on the experience and preferences of the choreographer and the director.

- **Choralography**: Combines the words "choral" and "choreography." Singers perform simple choreographed movements while singing, but their feet rarely move. Intended for a larger choral ensemble, this simplified choreography works well for massed choirs and big festival groups. Stevie Rivers was one of the first masters of this style of movement.

- **Arm-ography**: A word I invented for an excess amount of arm motions by a choral group; more of a cheerleading feel. Not necessarily a positive term.

- **Color pops**: The use of costumes to create visual excitement and "color pops" for the eye. Including color will complicate the choreography but can be very effective viewed from the house. More color pops (for example, each additional color of costume, prop or add-on) will make blocking more problematic for the choreographer.

- **Tableau**: A group of people attractively arranged, as if in a painting. Visually appealing, a tableau works well with ballad formations.

- **Ballady**: A nonsensical word I created to describe when an ensemble's members overact while performing a ballad. Singers are overdoing the emotions, leaning forward exaggerating the text more than necessary.

- **Bus talk**: The practice of not saying anything in public that could be misconstrued by another choir member, an instructor, or a parent. Save comments for the bus and, even then, keep comments on the positive side. Life is too short to pick apart other ensembles. Help set a good example in the performance world.

- **Reprise**: Pronounced *ruh-preeze*. Repetition of a musical theme; repeats an earlier part of the composition.

- **SRO:** Standing Room Only. The show is sold out! Something we all long to hear.

EDUCATING YOUR CHORAL ENSEMBLE
Ten "Be-Attitudes" for performers onstage and off

- **Be prepared.** Know what you are doing and where you are going. Be familiar with all entrances and exits. Make eye contact with audience members and other performers when entering and exiting the stage.

- **Be a performer.** The second you enter a stage, perform! You never get a second chance to make a first impression. Use great posture at all times and think stage presence. Be confident. Keep hands to sides unless choreographed otherwise. No picking and scratching (Kansas-speak). Don't adjust hair or costumes, or touch hands to the face. Someone is watching all the time.

- **Be a communicator.** Make sure you are understood. Be sure the articulation is precise. Don't forget about the middle and ending consonants. Going beyond clear enunciation, your facial responses should match the text. Communicate at every level.

- **Be sure to identify the goal.** Know what your ensemble is striving to achieve. The instructor should have explained the ensemble's purpose and mission. Know the goal and intent for each performance (entertaining, recruiting, or educating?). It is the performer's job to carry out the mission.

- **Be honest.** Audiences see through fake emoting and/or passive stage performances. Be energetic but not over the top with forged excitement. Entrances, transitions, and exits need sincerity and integrity.

- **Be versatile.** If something happens, don't panic onstage. Life happens. It will continue to happen on the stage. Be flexible and adaptable. The best performers are resourceful when something goes wrong.

- **Be artistic.** Don't be afraid to show your true colors. Then, experiment with new colors. Never settle for second best. Sing, dance, and live life to its fullest.

- **Be a growing entertainer.** Demand growth from your fellow performers and your instructor. Learn all avenues of the performance. Be true to the style physically and vocally.

- **Be professional.** Demonstrate professionalism onstage and off by having the correct costume, hair, and makeup. Press and clean costumes regularly. Shine shoes, check for runs in hosiery, wear correct jewelry, be on time, and be prepared.

- **Be a team member.** Work hard individually so that when you come together as a team, you are not the weak link. Don't let one bad attitude affect your spirit or the spirit of those around you. Attitudes are contagious.

EDUCATING YOUR ADMINISTRATION

The strength of a show choir or music theater ensemble is in its high-energy performance and in the enthusiastic audience response. It takes money and support to have a top-notch music program, as it does for athletic teams, academic

> Show choirs can be great recruiting tools for the fine arts department and the school.

programs, faculty and administration. Music educators have the obligation to teach students and enable them with experiences to excel in a variety of choral styles. To close the door on American-made musical forms shuts out a large portion of the future's musical history. This is current music being created right now! Show choirs can be great recruiting tools for the fine arts department and the school. The ensembles can perform for the local community as well as functioning as a PR arm for the school.

EDUCATING YOUR PARENT AND SUPPORT GROUPS

Parent booster groups can be a real help, if the director has a vision for the support group and remains in control. Parents enjoy creating the best stage experience for their children. Some helpful parent booster handouts are available online and from other successful music programs. Check out what works best for your situation but be careful that the tail doesn't start wagging the dog.

Students have specific, protected rights regarding the release of certain records. Therefore, it is imperative that privacy guidelines are respected at all times.

I'M JUST SAYING...

> *Personally, I have seen both good and bad results from involved parenting. What a blessing to have parents offer assistance by providing water bottles and snacks, being supportive on the sidelines, helping with fundraising projects, decorating, and building sets. At the same time, if parents are reliving high school days, complaining about "unfair auditions," or spreading rumors, consider talking one on one with the parents to redirect this energy for more positive support.*

CONTINUING EDUCATION

Workshops, festivals, summer camps, master classes, musical shares with area schools, books, and attendance at musical theater performances are ways to stay current on what is happening in the choral world. Education is expensive but will be worth the price and sacrifice. Don't let the lack of finances, time, or vision prevent educational opportunities, as grants and scholarships are

available if you are seriously motivated in growing a program. Music educators are responsible for the teaching and training of the next generation of musicians and music educators alike. The Internet is a great tool but shouldn't substitute for live entertainment.

For various reasons, some wonderful workshops of the past are no longer available for music educators. Please take time to thank your local music dealer and publishing companies, as they expend time and energy to support and finance workshops and reading sessions. These opportunities enable teachers, students, family members, and the community to enjoy and learn about music all through the year. Many of the workshops, camps, and reading sessions are held in the summer, but others are held at state, regional and national music conventions.

The following organizations offer wonderful resources for the music educator with websites that include workshop information, scholarship opportunities, and materials.

- The National Association for Music Education (MENC)—*menc.org*
- American Choral Directors Association (ACDA)—*acda.org*
- National Association of Teachers of Singing (NATS)—*nats.org*
- The National Band Association (NBA)—*nationalbandassociation.org*
- Barbershop Harmony Society—*barbershop.org*
- America Sings! (John Jacobson)—*americasings.org*

ANNUAL SHOW CHOIR OR CHORAL SUMMER WORKSHOPS I HAVE ATTENDED:

▶ Butler Showchoir Showcase, El Dorado, Kansas—*butlershowchoirshowcase.com*
    Valerie Lippoldt Mack, Artistic Director

▶ Shawnee Press Music in the Mountains, East Stroudsburg, Pennsylvania—*musicmountains.com*
    Greg Gilpin, Creative Director of Shawnee Press' Educational Choral Department

▶ Showchoir Camps of America, Decatur, Illinois, and Tiffin, Ohio—*showchoircamps.com*
    Dwight Jordan and Sue Moninger, Directors

▶ Nebraska Showchoir Camp, Lincoln, Nebraska—*events.unl.edu*
    Peter Eklund, Director

▶ Arts Mission's Sing Out workshop, Durham, North Carolina—*artsmission.com*
    Annette Layman, Director

▶ The Southern Experience: Show Choir Camp, University of S. Mississippi, Hattiesburg, Mississippi—
    John Flanery, Director *john.flanery@usm.edu*

▶ VanderCook College of Music MECA Summer Choral Workshop, Chicago, Illinois—
    vandercook.edu/meca

"SHOE" BUSINESS IS TOUGH

Choosing music is perhaps the most difficult element of putting the SHOW in CHOIR. If the music is trite, simple, or uninspired, the students and audience will lose interest. Make wise selections. The musical scores might be considered equivalent to the curriculum and required textbooks. If you ask students for input, they'll name their own personal likes, not thinking of anyone else's interests. This is rarely a good plan: What is "hot" one day may not be so popular by the time it is performed. Find quality music that has a shelf life *and* depth in the lyrics and composition.

I appreciate Greg Gilpin, composer and arranger for Shawnee Press, and his philosophy for music. Greg is also the director of Shawnee Press Educational Publications for Hal Leonard Corporation, where he oversees the creation of the educational music products. He believes in making good financial and educational musical choices, and provides workshops throughout the year with ideas such as budget-stretching music and programming for success. Greg recommends selecting classic pop literature and selections that challenge the ensemble. He also suggests adding some musical twists every now and then by throwing in the unexpected. This will keep the director, the singers, and the audience on their toes.

Speaking of toes, recommending music selections for you would be like my trying to select shoes for you and your students. There are as many options in the music world as there are in the shoe world. When shopping for that perfect pair of shoes, you might consider if they are one of a kind, will stop traffic, and are comfortable; you'll also look at brand name, color, affordability, and so forth. Don't give up finding the perfect musical fit; be creative and find the right music that suits you and your students. As the old saying goes, "If the shoe fits ..."

> Don't give up finding the perfect musical fit; be creative and find the right music that suits you and your students.

The following websites offer musical ideas and make it easy to see what is new on the charts and when it will be available. Ordering music has never been simpler. The sites include many sample pages for those who need to look at a selection, and sample audios are available for many of the arrangements. Another nice feature is a rating of the difficulty level for individual numbers.

Shawnee Press, *shawneepress.com*
Hal Leonard, *halleonard.com*

Chapter 3 includes a section on themes and show programming and thus provides more guidelines and direction in selecting material. Remember, the printed score is the starting point. The music is the heart and sole—I mean *soul*—of the show. You are looking for material to put more SHOW in the show. Choosing a variety of music is definitely the first step. The music must have the right fit and feel. Now go shopping!

I'M JUST SAYING...

By the way, I can choose shoes much faster than I can select literature for my ensembles. Ladies, are you with me? Jimmy Choo stilettos— just for the record! On second thought, comfortable Ugg house slippers sound pretty nice after a long day of teaching. Tough choice! ☺

KNOW THE SCORE

Directors expect their singers to know the score musically and to make continuous improvements each rehearsal. Before the first musical run-through, the director must do his or her homework by studying the score and knowing it inside and out, front to back, and every note in between. The music is the core of the show choir and is the heartbeat and pulse of the show or concert. The better prepared you are in teaching the score, the faster and more efficiently your students will learn. Rehearsals will be less stressful and more fun for everyone involved.

How can students be expected to sing perfectly if the director doesn't have a concept of the perfect sound? Here are some tips for directors to come up with that sound and to really **KNOW THE SCORE.**

THE SCOREBOARD

- Make sure you can **live with the literature** for several weeks (or months or a semester). Some songs are fun to hear once, but repeatedly is a different story.

- **Play through each part and the accompaniment** on a keyboard. If you can't sight-read, ask an accompanist to help you play through all the parts. If you don't have keyboard skills, it is never too late to start learning. Confidence at the keyboard gives you a sense of security as you face your choir.

- **Circle any mistakes you make as you sight-read**. If a section of music gives you trouble, your students will have twice the trouble in the rehearsal.

- Settle on **breathing and phrasing in the music and mark notation** accordingly. It may seem obvious, but when 50 pairs of eyes are staring at you, you'll be thankful you took the time to make marks ahead of time.

- Decide where the softest and loudest sections should be and **highlight those sections**. Sometimes color coding helps organize your thoughts. If you mark it the same for every piece of music, it becomes second nature and you'll know where you are on the page, even if you can't always see the text. You'll read in color.

- Use a **red pencil for the text**. Check the next section to find more ideas for studying lyrics.

- **Research the history of the piece**. Know about the composer and lyricist and why the piece was composed. Students love learning personal trivia and realizing they share trials and tribulations with famous musicians, not to mention gaining the knowledge that the musicians survived their teenage years and were able to write and sometimes fantasize about their journeys.

- Be able to **explain what was happening in the time period** when the piece was composed. Students will better relate to a composition after knowing some of the history.

- **Draw a pair of eyeglasses** a measure or two before the most difficult section(s) of the piece. Whether it is a problem with rhythm, intervals, or diction, the glasses will get your attention.

- Guess what!? **You now know the score**. You are prepared to teach efficiently and confidently.

I'M JUST SAYING...

I confess I am a "fan-ilow." Yes, I am a Barry Manilow enthusiast. One of my friends, Kye Brackett, sings backup for Mr. Manilow. I was even more impressed when, after a concert I attended, Mr. Manilow called Kye and told him it was time for notes. To me, the concert was pure perfection. Kye proceeded to tell me that Mr. Manilow strives for flawless performances and calls rehearsals regularly to improve the score. "Copacabana" just keeps getting better. And that, my friends, is why I love Barry Manilow! ♥

THE TEXT

In July 1984, I had the privilege of studying with Fred Waring, "the man who taught America to sing." Many of the lessons I teach my own students stem from the instruction I received from my time in Pennsylvania. Mr. Waring, who invented a system called *Tone Syllables* that is still in use today, is quoted as saying, "Sing *all* the beauty of *all* the sounds of *all* the syllables of *all* the words, and interpret accordingly."

It would be difficult to briefly explain the tone syllable method as Mr. Waring wrote prolifically on the subject. His work can be found through many sources, including Shawnee Press, the publishing company he created in Pennsylvania in the late 1930s. Mr. Waring also backed the invention of the Waring Blendor and directed vocal groups called The Pennsylvanians and The Waring Blendors. Bottom line? The text is important. If you don't think so, ask an audience member or an instrumentalist!

SOME IDEAS ON STUDYING THE TEXT WITH YOUR STUDENTS

- **Relate the lyrics to something personal** in the students' lives. Discuss in class or ask the students to do as a writing assignment if something is too personal to share with class members.

- Ask one student to **read the text as a poem.** Keeping class members involved, take turns expounding on the meaning of the poem.

- Using the **Robert Shaw technique of count-singing**, ask half the singers to count while the other half reads or sings the text. Switch the readers and the counters. (Count-singing is a valuable rehearsal technique created by Shaw, a student of Fred Waring's. The two believed that diction and rhythm take center stage. The goal is to increase rhythmic accuracy and togetherness with the lyrics.)

- If **singing a foreign language, ask students to write the exact translation** above each word. The translations provided in the scores are usually close but not exact. For example, the King James version of the Bible is paraphrased from the Greek Bible and is not an exact translation.

- **Try the onomatopoeia technique** with certain words and treat them accordingly. Onomatopoeia is the naming of a thing or action by a vocal imitation of the associated sound. Some of my favorite onomatopoeia words are *smack, zing, buzz, moo, tick-tock, purr, clap, flutter, splash, poof, hiss,* and *hum.* Ask choir members their favorite words, and then ask the singers to interpret them vocally, making the text come alive.

- When using **pop diction, be careful not to sound too affected**. Diction should sound natural. Implode rather than explode certain ending consonants. Sing as you would speak, deciding whether to use vernacular or formalized diction.

- Using a **red pencil as you read the text,** underline the part of the word or the words that should be stressed in each sentence. Do not emphasize every word. Listen carefully.

- Use **facial expressions** to enhance the text.

- Experiment with **singing the lyrics with various accents while discovering tall vowels.** Then, unify the text.

- Dig into the **emotion of the lyrics**. Start with a ballad or a country number. You will be sure to have a text about love or about lost love. Either way, think about getting deeper into the story line. Is there a subtext or second layer of emotions?

I'M JUST SAYING...

Included in my book **Icebreakers: 60 Fun Activities That Will Build a Better Choir** *is an activity that demonstrates vocal inflections and the text. The object of "Say oh!" is to teach students there are many ways to respond depending on the situation. The inflection of your reply would be different when told you'd won the $100,000 sweepstakes compared to your response hearing that your dog had just died. Your reaction is still different when hearing that your dad was wearing his embarrassing Hawaiian shirt in public. See how the power of the text can affect the sound!*

WARM-UPS

It goes without saying: Before going onstage, singers need to vocalize and dancers need to physically stretch. Without properly warming up, injuries occur. Our performers need to be in the habit of stretching their voices and bodies so they can achieve even more on and off the stage. Here are a few favorite warm-ups.

VOCAL WARM-UPS (VOCAL-"EASES")

1) **Breath temperature exercise.** Check the warmth of your breath by putting your hand in front of your mouth. Is the breath warm or cool as you exhale? Clue: If you're breathing properly, the breath will be warm. No shallow breathing.

2) **Ratio exercise.** Inhale through your nose for one second; hold for four seconds; exhale out for two seconds. Keeping the same ratio, increase the amount of time (2:8:4, 3:12:6, 10:40:20, and beyond). This is an ideal exercise to do before exams as it pumps blood through the body and recharges the mind. I use this exercise before each and every performance to calm nerves and focus the performers.

3) **Humming exercise.** Hum and move jaws like a cow chewing its cud (a Kansas image here). This exercise rids the jaw of tension. Turn to your right and carefully massage the shoulders of the person in front of you.

4) **Lip trill exercise** (rolling R's) and lip buzzes (like a five-year-old playing with a toy tractor).

5) "I *love* to sing." Throw a Frisbee on the octave (1-8-5-3-1). You can alter the words to "I *live* to sing" or "I *have* to sing" and pantomime tossing roses or confetti in the air.

6) **Diction exercises**. Get articulators working as you foster a smiling choir and a focused attitude with these ideas. Hold a tongue twister contest with your students to find the best tongue twister and award a prize.

- ♪ "The lips, the teeth, the tip of the tongue"—use any pattern of notes.
- ♪ "Unique New York" or "toy boat"—sing each phrase on a pitch and travel up the scale.
- ♪ "Cinnamon lemon liniment" up the scale and "red leather, yellow leather" back down.
- ♪ "Girl gargoyle, guy gargoyle, girl, guy gargoyle."
- ♪ "One small fellow, he felt smart." (Careful with this one. Not for the timid or middle school!)

    A palindrome is a word or phrase that can be sung the same way in either direction. "Sit on a potato pan Otis" (5 notes up and down, syllables continue to change in the pattern) is an example of that.

Check out these invaluable vocal warm-up resources published by Shawnee Press:

**115 Tang Tungling Tongue Twisters
from A to Z!**
Greg Gilpin

**The Perfect Blend: Over 100 Seriously
Fun Vocal WARM-UPS**
Tim Seelig

PHYSICAL WARM-UPS (DANCE-"ERCIZES")

- Yoga exercises: These stabilize the core and remind singers to simultaneously breathe and sing correctly.
- Perfect jumping jacks: The leader states how many will be done. If anyone does extra, the group repeats the exercise, adding more perfect jumping jacks each time. Count out loud!
- Perfect posture: Stand with shoulders against a wall or lie on the floor to check posture. Check back breathing by placing hands on the back to see if the back muscles are functioning correctly. Better yet, lie on the floor, putting your head on another person's stomach. Everyone says "ha" and keeps adding a "ha" – great breath and posture exercise all combined into one.
- Push-ups, sit-ups, and dancing planks: Learn to use the core and chest muscles properly. Our singers are part athletes. Want the same budget as the football team? Work hard physically and don't complain.

> If the choir is singing without energy and "going through the motions," stop the rehearsal and have the ensemble take a lap around the building. Fresh air/oxygen can do wonders for a nonproductive rehearsal.

I'M JUST SAYING...

Instruct students to stretch both arms into the air as high as they can. As students do this, tell them to stretch higher (which they will). Ask two more times to stretch higher. Most of them will be able to do so with a few grunts and groans. Why didn't they do this initially? The first time, you asked them to stretch as high as they could, and yet they were able to stretch higher several more times after that. Why is that? What were they saving for? This is a great lesson and students will quickly understand the lack of giving 100 percent in rehearsals. Thank you to master educator Paul Gulsvig of Onalaska, Wisconsin, for this enlightening exercise.

VOCAL VS. MOVEMENT

Music theater provides 65 to 75 percent of the available jobs in music performance. The show choir trains the singer for this venue. Movement and good singing go hand in hand. By now you have gathered the importance of solid vocal production. The music is at the center of the show and is what makes the show tick. The visual is often impaired by vocal problems, and in turn the choreography can detract from vocals. If an ensemble looks amazing but doesn't have a solid vocal sound, the ensemble will *never* be top-notch. If an ensemble has incredible vocals but lacks in dancing skills, *there is hope*—seriously. I've learned those truths over the years as an adjudicator for state, regional, and national competitions and festivals.

Simply put, emphasize beautiful and healthy singing at all times. As a music professor, a choreographer, and someone who has been in charge of all aspects of the show, I have developed my own survival tricks.

COMBINING VISUAL ART WITH MUSICAL ART

- Add choreography once the ensemble has the **song completely memorized**. The dynamics, phrasing, intonation, and style must also be memorized.

- Be sure **the visual and the vocals line up**. When the two are in sync, students will memorize the choreography faster and reinforce the memorization of the text.

- Learn techniques in **choreography that will crescendo the movements** and tie into the vocals. Even beginning groups can have amazing dynamic contrasts with this subtle trick. One illustration: When the singers are singing softly, place them upstage in a "blob" formation, sitting close together. As the music swells, choreograph the students to stand up, a few at a time, until everyone is standing. At a key change or a dramatic musical section, instruct the singers to step forward and spread out. Even if the dynamics don't change, the movements will look stronger visually and it will appear to the audience as if the choir is singing louder. Magic!

- Separate words and **sing in a marcato style** when performing music that is up-tempo. The audience will understand the lyrics and the singers will be understood over the band.

- Use **strong consonants**. Spit words to the very back of the room.

- Remember **middle consonants**. Directors typically ask choirs to emphasize the beginning and endings of words, but often forget to call attention to the middle consonants. Words sound mushy and diction is not clear when these consonants are ignored. At the same time, not all consonants are equal. Decide how the word should be pronounced and insist the singers pronounce the word as instructed. Barbershop quartets have understood the importance of the concept for years. Play excerpts of an award-winning barbershop performance. The 2009 International Barbershop Chorus champions, The Ambassadors of Harmony, have an exciting rendition of "76 Trombones" that can be viewed on their website, *aoh.org*. Who knows, it might inspire your guys to start their own quartet.

- A **musical-ballad trick is to push the tempo slightly** at the climax of the piece. If your group is up to the challenge, try an *a cappella* section in the middle of the piece. Let the combo drop out. Keep the bass underneath. Students will feel accomplished and the audience will enjoy the range of diversity in the accompaniment.

- Let the **instrumentalists assist with dynamic contrast**. If you're using live musicians, this is an easy assignment. Ask the instrumentalists to play louder during dance breaks as this helps build the bigger musical sections. If the band exaggerates the dynamics (within reason), this expands the dynamic range for the overall program. If you're using a taped accompaniment, an experienced sound person can duplicate this effect.

- **Experiment with eurhythmics** when working with any choral group. As the choir sings, instruct the members to step to the music, walking in a large circle around the room. Voice teachers use the concept of moving while singing as it gets rid of tension in the voice and body. This technique will greatly improve the musicianship of each and every vocalist.

- **Respect the material.** Trust the vehicle you have chosen and prepare for the journey by doing your homework. The path won't be easy, but you will eventually get there if you keep the faith and believe in yourself and your ensemble. First, you must believe.

- **The music needs to fit the ensemble**. The ensemble does not have to do every repeat, every verse, or every chorus. If you need additional time to get the choir on the risers, double the introduction. Composers and arrangers write for a large generic population. If you're taking a piece to contest or a festival, simply mark your scores to give the adjudicators visual indication of the changes.

The brilliant and witty Fritz Mountford, author, arranger, and former vocal coach and consultant for Walt Disney theme parks, always referred to purchasing music as buying a can of green beans from the store. Sometimes you might feel like eating the green beans straight from the can. But if you are headed to the Lutheran church's potluck dinner, you will add the can of mushroom soup, the dried onions on top, and a few secret ingredients to make it your own, and then place it in the prettiest casserole dish you can find—complete with matching hot pads. The printed music is the starting place and it is your job to make the music come off the page. Each year reflects different needs and requirements. Time crunches, budget issues, tenor shortages, and lack of accompanists are real issues. Every year is unique, and master teachers know what ingredients are needed, how to blend it all together, and what new combination is required for a recipe of success.

I'M JUST SAYING...

This activity is hands-on and your students will have an immediate "a-ha" reaction. Videotape a performance/rehearsal. Bring a TV monitor to the next rehearsal. Instruct students to write positive and constructive comments regarding the performance. Assign the students to watch only their own movements and to take notes only on themselves. This will allow self-assessment and not foster bad relations by critiquing thy neighbor.

First, watch the piece with the volume turned off, allowing the students to closely focus their observations on the movement. Is the choreography clean and does it convey the intended message? Then, turn off or hide the picture, turn up the volume, and replay the recording. Now the students are listening carefully to the aural portion of the show. Are the lyrics understandable? How is the diction? What improvements need to be made?

Collect the papers and choose a few comments from each to read aloud. Later in the semester, return the comments to the performers. Students are excited to see their "expert critique" of themselves and the show. The students have ownership in the project; they are actively listening and watching the show as well as using critical skills to critique. If writing assignments are required in your school, this exercise may double as a cocurricular assignment.

CHAPTER 2:
AUDITIONING

THE AUDITION

"There she is … Miss America!" OK, so I'm no Bert Parks, but I have had the privilege of accompanying several Miss Kansas contestants to the Miss America pageant as a talent coach. Each year fifty-three of the most beautiful young ladies in the country audition for the job of being Miss America; yet on that Saturday night, in front of millions of people, only one of them "wins" the audition and takes home the crown. Time after time I am frustrated by the same thing: Fifty-two contestants leave the pageant feeling like losers because there is only <u>one</u> "winner." Each and every girl worked hard to get there, improved in talent, physical appearance, and mental awareness, and raised money for a cause of her choice. Why, then, don't they all feel like winners?

My dilemma with the Miss America pageant is still unresolved; I have, however, made some changes in my own auditioning practices and in my adjudication for national show choir competitions. Educate your students long before the audition.

FIVE IDEAS FOR THOSE AUDITIONING

- Know exactly **what you are auditioning for** and then **practice, practice, practice until you feel overprepared.**

- **No excuses**. Period. The panel gets tired of hearing excuses about allergies, missing pitch pipes, music being in the wrong key, or whatever. The judges can hear talent through phlegm and know if the person is right for the part. Get in the room and do your best. No excuses!

- Be **professional** in every aspect of the audition. Print your name clearly; be on time; look the part or dress accordingly; and do exactly what is asked of you, nothing more and nothing less.

> **Be professional in every aspect of the audition.**

- **Remain positive** throughout the audition.

- **Thank the accompanist, the teacher, and anyone else assisting with the auditions.** Your actions might be recorded or watched in the waiting room. I have a great anecdote from Rich Taylor, who spent years working for the Walt Disney Company, where his roles included watching auditions and doing casting. A talented performer seemed a shoe-in to land the job, but another Disney employee witnessed the performer's rude and unprofessional behavior (criticizing the accompanist and sending out a stream of cuss words) in the parking lot. That is one way to lose a Disney contract!

IDEAS FOR THOSE ON THE OTHER SIDE OF THE TABLE (THE AUDITIONING PANEL)

1) **The first volunteer gets to sing last as well**. Because very few people want to volunteer to sing first, this offer will speed up the process. Normally many will enthusiastically volunteer, as they know they will get two attempts to impress.

2) **Music instructors should always use a panel and videotape.** Do this for your safety and protection.

3) **Reaudition soloists, ensembles, and section leaders regularly** whether that is each year, semester, or performance. Reauditioning keeps students on their toes and up on their craft. Currently, I direct and choreograph the Butler Headliners at Butler Community College in El Dorado, Kansas. I reaudition the singer/dancers each semester. I look at grades, attendance, attitude, and contribution to the ensemble for continued membership in the ensemble. This reminds the performers that membership in the Butler Headliners is a privilege and not a right and that they must continue growing and improving to maintain membership in the select ensemble. Many times, directors place students in an ensemble as a freshman and then that student knows he or she has a guaranteed spot in the group until graduation. I highly recommend the reauditioning process for many reasons. As with all auditions, use a panel of judges, videotape the actual audition, and document all portions of the audition process. Another of my favorite quotes is "Today's 10 is tomorrow's 2." You have to keep improving, because everyone else around you is working hard.

4) **Don't postpone posting** the list because you're afraid of hurting feelings. Rejection is a part of life. Students need to learn how to deal with getting, and not getting, the part.

5) Ask students to **audition with a verse and chorus from a ballad as well as from an up-tempo selection.** Students will sing various styles differently and need contrasting pieces to demonstrate their abilities.

DON'T JUST *SHOW* UP AT THE AUDITION

TOP FIFTY TRIED-AND-TRUE TALENT TIPS FOR AUDITIONS

1) **Music should be in a three-ring binder** in nonglare plastic sleeves or printed on card stock. It is good to buy multiple copies of music.

2) All **cuts in the music should be marked clearly**, including ending notes, any tempo or key changes, and repeats. Discuss politely with the accompanist prior to the audition.

3) Even though you are singing 32 bars, **know the whole song**. Many times, you may be asked to sing more. Be prepared.

4) **Know the table of contents, the style, era, composer facts**. Again—be prepared.

5) **Bring a minimum of two songs of every style**. That could include a representative of every major composer and each decade of pop/rock. Bring classics and new pieces, but avoid material currently on Broadway.

6) **An up-tempo piece and a comic selection** need to be your bread and butter. Bring a character number to showcase your personality and your voice.

7) **Don't sing material from the show you are auditioning for** unless instructed to do so.

8) **Bring an eight-inch-by-ten-inch color headshot** with you to the audition. A headshot should always show the "fun" you, not a serious side. Smile for the photo and show your teeth. If you are auditioning as a dancer, you will need a full body shot in dancewear or something that shows off the body. Singers need shots that are three-fourths body or shoulder up.

9) Be sure your **photo is current and looks like you**. No silly shots from Facebook. Invest in a good, professional headshot. It is usually cost efficient to make several copies at a time. Be prepared for the next audition.

10) **Staple a professional-looking bio on the back** of your headshot. Paperclips fall off, as do sticky notes.

11) All resumes should be in black and white and easy to follow. **Don't get cutesy** when putting your bio together.

12) **Always bring extra headshots/resumes** to the audition and tailor them to the audition.

13) Rule of thumb—**don't go back more than five years on a resume**. Normally a one-page bio is sufficient. Let your talent speak for itself.

14) **Resumes should include a contact e-mail and cell phone number**. Don't provide personal information unless you know the person, instructor, or company's reputation.

15) **If you're doing multiple auditions at a venue, do not change hairstyles and clothing between auditions**. Look the same for each audition so the panel remembers you. Bring a dance bag with various dance shoes as the director may ask for a variety of dance styles.

16) **Select age-appropriate material**. Don't select "Dance 10, Looks 3" from *A Chorus Line* if you are a middle school girl. This piece might be up-tempo and fun to sing, but is not appropriate at this time of your life. The material must be suitable for the singer.

17) No matter how much you love singing along with Kristin Chenoweth in your car, it is generally **not a good idea to audition with songs from mega-popular shows**. If you do, you will be setting yourself up for comparison with the stars who have won Tony awards.

18) **Find songs that you can identify with on some level**. Think of particular portions of the lyrics (or subtext) that are meaningful to you.

19) **Be real and make honest choices throughout the audition**. Your own personal style and what you bring to the stage are what make your audition unique and memorable. Master the technique first, and then add your own flair.

20) **While you're in the process of growing and improving, focus on your best features**. If you are concerned that you might look too old for the part of Annie, resist the temptation to wear heavy makeup, heels, and a leotard to the audition.

21) Ladies, **look professional with skirts that fall at the knees**. Big hair is almost always a bad idea. Look clean. Wear makeup but **don't stylize yourself**.

22) **Men, ties are a good option at auditions**. For a more casual look, wear a T-shirt under a sports coat. One dressy item and one casual item is a good rule of thumb for males.

23) **Don't close your eyes on the ballad** or act "ballady." Your eyes communicate the lyrics.

24) **Practice what you preach.** "Get Happy." "This is the Moment." "Don't Stop Believin'!"

25) **Do not make excuses** or run to your car or locker for items that you should have had with you. No excuses ever! **Be prepared**.

26) **Arrive early**. If you audition early in the day, chances are you will get a longer audition.

27) **If you can't arrive early, try to audition right after lunch**. Judges are always happier after a meal.

28) **Build a rapport with the judges**. Don't speak unless spoken to, but find out about the judging panel and speak intelligently to anyone on the panel.

29) If a monitor doesn't do it for you, **announce what you will be singing**. If the panel asks you to choose a number, select an up-tempo, funny song—if it is your best 16 bars.

30) **Let the accompanist know you value his or her talent and time**. Say thanks and tell the accompanist how much you enjoyed the collaboration.

31) **Minimize page turns for the accompanist.** Buy extra copies to cut and paste music for easy page turns.

32) **Never look directly at the panel**; look above them. Direct gazes will make them feel awkward.

33) **Check your e-mail and cell phone messages daily**. Failing to stay in communication will appear irresponsible. Adjudicators/teachers/employers do communicate, and word will get around if you are not reliable and professional. It's called show *business* for a reason.

34) **Include a short cover letter with the application**. Be positive and professional in your writing—and be sure to proofread before sending.

35) **Keep growing**. Take every dance class, voice lesson, and acting class. Audition all you can.

36) **Breathe, and congratulate yourself**. Winners don't back away from the possibility of failure. The fact that you prepared and completed the audition sets you apart from all those who shied away from the opportunity.

37) Waiting to hear? The road is long. If this audition didn't work, **there will be plenty of other opportunities down the road**.

38) Nerves are good. The **nervous energy will give you the extra edge** you need in the audition.

39) You may not look the part. This part may not be right for you. But **do a good job and you may be asked back** to audition or be selected for another part in the future. There are gazillions of other parts for those who prepare and continue to audition.

40) **Be confident but not cocky.** Don't step over the line with arrogance. Leave your ego at the door. Your talent will speak for itself. And remember, in auditions and in life … big hat, no cattle.

41) **Remain focused**—no matter what.

42) Before an audition, **prepare with an actual dress rehearsal**. Rehearse in the shoes and the outfit, making sure the piece is memorized and the cuts are correct. Videotape the "dress rehearsal" and see if you (acting as a judge on the auditioning panel) would hire you (the person on the video recording). You will learn a great deal from this activity.

43) **Let your face reflect the message** of the song.

44) **Be in shape physically.** Don't be out of breath after running up two flights of stairs for the audition.

45) **Bring a dance bag** to the audition with various dance shoes.

46) **Give yourself time** to prepare, and ALWAYS plan ahead.

47) **Be honest with yourself and your work ethic**. If you get the same answer time after time, it is TIME for you to do some soul-searching and re-evaluating. Maybe there is another line of work in the performance field that is perfect for you.

48) When finished, **thank everyone for their time**. Men, hold the door for the female monitor and use gentleman manners. Ladies, be gracious and polite.

49) Prepare so you **have no regrets**.

50) **Follow up with a handwritten thank-you note** in a timely fashion.

> **Prepare so you have no regrets.**

SCHOLARSHIP AUDITIONS

I get a lot of questions about auditioning for college. Students who are successful in high school want to know how and when to set up college fine arts admission or scholarship auditions. It is imperative that students get the correct information, ask and audition early on in the process, and know how to prepare. Here is some advice to help you reach your goal.

COLLEGE FINE ARTS ADMISSION AND SCHOLARSHIP AUDITION INFORMATION

1) **Mark your calendars now**! Unless a college encourages setting up an individual audition time, it is best to adhere to the prescheduled date. When college personnel are prepared for your visit, they are better able to meet and greet you, answer your questions, and give you the personal attention you want and need. Don't reschedule or miss your audition.

2) **Get the facts**. Communicate with each college department before you arrive on campus. Be sure you're properly prepared to perform to your greatest potential. Ask about the audition procedure: Is an accompanist provided? Will you be taking a techniques class? Is an individual audition piece required? What are the other guidelines? How many monologues are required? Know what you will be doing and where you are going *before* arriving on the campus.

3) **Set the perfect tone**. Being properly dressed for the audition will increase your comfort factor and make the right first impression. Look professional and allow the faculty to assess you properly. Ladies, be sure to wear some makeup but don't overdo it. Please be modest. Gentlemen, wear nice pants, a shirt, a tie, dress shoes, and dark socks. Do not wear flip-flops or sunglasses for a dance audition as neither is safe nor professional. If you are given a name tag to wear, display it securely at shoulder level. Do not chew gum. Put away your cell phone. Most important, give the teacher your undivided attention and respect.

4) **Put yourself in the best light**. A willingness to try sight-reading exercises or to pick up new movements or acting techniques demonstrates an open mind. Do not exhibit bad habits in technique or in attitude. Follow directions and instructions without being told twice. If the panel asks you to step up to the table, do just that. Don't shake hands or offer any extra information.

5) **Take notes**. Auditioning on campus gives you the opportunity to speak with students and learn about campus life. Get names of alums you could contact at a later date if you still have questions. Students are generally open and honest about their college and musical experiences.

6) **Cram for the test**. Learn all about the school and make notes about what YOU want to learn when you attend. Remember that the audition process is a two-way street. You are interviewing the faculty as they interview you. Decide what you want in a school and use these answers to evaluate whether the program meets your needs. Be sure you understand the philosophy of the department. Don't assume anything.

7) **Think $$$!** Check out financial aid. When making preliminary inquiries about degrees offered, academic curriculum, campus life, and financial aid, ask about other available scholarships. Audition early, as money decreases as the semester wanes. College programs must also invest wisely and consider budgets.

8) **Extend your reach**. You may be able to audition for scholarships in activities you never dreamed possible. Every college is unique and looks for various traits in auditioning students. But just because you don't qualify at one place, don't be afraid to audition for another department or at another school.

9) **"Never think never."** Don't give up but do figure out how to work smarter and harder. Oftentimes, faculty members are more impressed by positive attributes and important life skills than simply by a person's talent. Be prompt, considerate, excited to participate, and ready to give 100 percent. Be a good citizen. It is amazing the good things that will happen to you when you avoid shortcuts and step out in the right direction.

10) **Ask the right questions and get the answers you need**. It is better to question school officials before experiencing hidden costs or learning of expectations that were not set out from the beginning.

> **Ask the right questions and get the answers you need.**

11) **Find faculty members you want to emulate** and have as role models. Identify excellent instructors who will motivate you and sculpt your talents. Discover and gravitate to people with balanced lives. Find colleges with balanced programs. Be wary of individuals who assume they have all the answers and don't want you to study with or learn from any other person or source.

12) **Work on time-managing skills and adhering to a budget**. Many college freshmen fail because of an inadequacy in one or both of these skills. The student then has to live with the grades he or she received from one semester of bad choices. These grades will stay on transcripts forever. To be successful, a college student may need to grow up overnight.

13) **Leave a clean trail**. Just like running for a political office, your Internet presence reflects on you as a person. Be careful of what is posted about you on Facebook and other social media sites. The Internet is called the worldwide web for a reason. Once posted, words can never be taken back.

14) **Expect college to be different from high school.** Plan ahead. You will not be able to ease into college if you want to be successful. Make good decisions from the get-go. Immediate transformation is the key.

15) **Keep a sense of humor and enjoy the process**. Remember, you can always transfer to another college, university, or program if you decide the college or program isn't right for you. But strive to do your best. If you are serious about doing the right thing, you will be successful regardless of the school. If you do end up transferring, a strong record will only help.

"Unless you try to do something beyond what you have already mastered, you will never grow."
—Ralph Waldo Emerson

I'M JUST SAYING...

Life is not fair. Tell me about it! I'm sure you all have similar stories. As I am writing this, my best church choir tenor (we've volunteered side by side for the past fourteen years) has stomach cancer and has been given two to four months to live. Talk about a godly man with an amazing attitude and spirit. The same day of his diagnosis, we learned that a former student was denied an adoption for the fourth time after being assured the adoption would go through. She and her husband would be incredible parents and have prayed for a child for several years. Now that is not fair. Put it in perspective!

And on a lighter note …
A few years ago, one of my former students traveled to New York to audition for American Idol. *He saved his earnings all semester to pay for the trip. After standing in line for literally two days, he finally had his turn on stage. He was told he had twenty seconds to sing his* a cappella *audition. He paused to collect his breath and think of his starting pitch. Before he uttered a sound, the producer yelled "Next!" and that was it. Moral of the story? I'm not sure—but I do know that life is not always fair. Make the most of it while you can. His experience does, however, make a great story for this section on auditioning.*

THE AUDIENCE

This section of the book is about knowing your audience. I am serious about audience etiquette and feel that "theater manners" are not being taught, caught, or enforced anymore. Maybe I'm a little old-fashioned, but it saddens me to see the loss of respect from "the audience" at movies, high school and college productions, and even church events. Cell phone etiquette is something new for this generation to figure out. Recently I attended a wedding ceremony, and a guest not only answered her cell in the middle of the vows but proceeded to have a full out-and-out disagreement with her ex-boyfriend.

Since you've made it this far into the book, I will now share one of my most embarrassing moments with you. My family has seen me stick my foot in my mouth many times so this story is nothing out of the ordinary. Notice I said *one* of my embarrassing moments. Stick with me; there'll be more stories, I promise!

So, I had tickets to see the Broadway production of *Movin' Out.* Now to some of you, that may not sound like a big deal. But to this little ol' Kansas girl, it was huge. I actually made time in my schedule, had tickets in hand (OK, back-row seats, but I was in the house), and was in New York City! I was thrilled at the prospect of seeing the work from the creative choreographer and Tony-winner Twyla Tharp. To see her inventive choreography and to hear Billy Joel's music … well, let's just say I was in heaven.

In the middle of Act II, a man in a hat and overcoat walked in and rudely stood next to my seat on the aisle. This man was anxiously pacing back and forth. Quite out of character, I angrily signaled to him to sit down and I even did the little "hmm–mm" cough all the while glaring at him. I was angry that this man was ruining the theater experience. Not making much of an impact, I finally shook my index finger at him and shushed him in a rather loud voice. Luckily for us (and him), the show was ending and the performers were taking their bows. As we stood with the audience for the standing ovation, the man ripped off his coat and bolted to the stage. Imagine my surprise when he jumped on stage and started singing "New York State of Mind." Yep, it was none other than Billy Joel himself. And I gave him the "mom finger." That was one night I didn't stick around to ask for autographs!

I'M JUST SAYING...

On a less embarrassing and different kind of "moving" note
Each Christmas I take my show choir to carol around town. We conclude the day at the area nursing home. It is important for students to have a variety of audiences and know how to behave and react to each audience—no matter how small or seemingly unappreciative. One of the patients at the home, a 92-year-old woman, had not spoken or uttered a sound in the four years she had been living there. She was not able to communicate at all. When the Headliners started singing "Silent Night," some of the patients chimed in. Tears began rolling down the woman's cheeks and for the first time in four years, she actually sang along. The nurses and the attendants were shocked and tears were streaming down their faces as well. The language and sharing of music made all the difference. Many lives were changed after the singing that afternoon. I'm glad we didn't stick with the usual audience. Who is your greatest audience? Are you sure?

PROPER THEATER ETIQUETTE

A LIST TO SHARE WITH YOUR STUDENTS BEFORE THEY ATTEND A THEATER OR MUSIC EVENT

- **Dress appropriately** when attending a performance. You will be treated with respect when you look and act in a professional manner. Please do not enter the venue in costume.

> You will be treated with respect when you look and act in a professional manner.

- **Remove hats** during performances. The wearing of hats is discourteous to the performers as well as to audience members.

- **Arrive early**. Do not enter the theater during the performance. Wait until applause or until the ushers open the doors. If you must enter the theater, move quickly and quietly, without interrupting what is happening on stage.

- **Turn off all cell phones, watches, and pagers** during the performance. Cell phones are absolutely not allowed during the performance. No texting of any type during the show. The cell phone glow is distracting for the performers as well as for audience members nearby.

- **Keep your feet on the floor and not propped on the back of the seat in front of you,** whether it is vacant or not.

- **Enter at the end of the row**; do not step over seats. Be polite when moving to and from seats.

- **Do not bring food or drink into the theater**. If you must unwrap hard candy or cough drops, please do so during applause or intermission.

- **No talking (or whispering) during a performance**. When you are talking, it bothers the performers and audience members alike. Please don't sing along with the performers. Have a great time, but remember that those around you are trying to enjoy the performance as well.

- The only time you should **leave during a performance is in the event of an emergency.**

- **Applaud at the end of the performance** during the curtain call. Do not yell individual names or make catcalls or whoop and holler. This is a fine arts event and not a sporting event.

- At the conclusion of the performance, **wait for the house lights before exiting.**

- **Refrain from any negative discussions or comments** about performers or performances. Find positive things to say. Think the "golden rule" at all times.

- **THANK YOU.** When you are using proper music theater etiquette, you and those around you will truly enjoy the live theater experience.

I'M JUST SAYING...

Our fine arts department has tried numerous approaches to get proper theater etiquette instilled in our scholarship students. As educators we want to encourage theater attendance and appreciation of live theater. At the same time we would like to teach our students correct protocol in the "house." It seems many audience members could use a dose of these theater etiquette rules. Listing rules in the program may not be the answer. The best solution? As a precurtain speech, invite a small child to explain the house rules and how to be polite during the show. It is incredible the amount of respect that will be shown to the youngster. It works even better if the child is part of the show and in costume. Don't believe me? Try it. (Dimples and toothless grins are helpful!)

Comedy is another means to get the message across. On a recent flight, the passengers in the plane were clearly annoyed and started to ignore the flight attendants when they began giving instructions. But when humor was used in the speech, the passengers couldn't help but listen, as they didn't want to miss a word of the clever instructions. "The captain is assisted by First Officer Justin Case. In the unlikely event that this flight will be turned into a cruise, pull out your life vest." Passengers will be playing close attention, trust me!

THE REHEARSAL

What kills most rehearsals? Why are choirs not ready to perform? Why do students dread going to choir rehearsals? The answer is …

Well, let me tell you a story. I have a tap teacher in California whom I absolutely love. His tap classes are totally amazing and I would travel many miles to take one of his master tap classes. I learned something very valuable from him. He taught me that if you want to tap faster, you … *get ready for this … it will blow your mind!* What is the answer to wanting to tap faster? You … *OK, here it is, drum roll, please …* The answer to wanting to tap faster … is to simply … TAP FASTER!

If you want a better rehearsal, quit talking and REHEARSE! I am as guilty as the next director, as I love to share all the funny and "brilliant" things said by my own two children, hear movie reviews from the students, and place my bets on the cafeteria's lunch mystery meat. Every rehearsal needs some chitchat and icebreakers before class. But when the bell rings or the clock strikes "time," be ready to REHEARSE!

TWENTY TIME-TESTED IDEAS FOR RUNNING SMOOTH REHEARSALS

1) **Start and end rehearsals on time**. It is disrespectful to make students late for other activities and classes.

2) **Be organized**. Put the daily POA (plan of action) on the board or in their folders.

3) **Say it once**. Students need to get in the habit of listening.

4) One of my favorite rehearsal rules is concerning cell phones. **No phones in class**. If someone forgets and a cell phone rings, the students all yell "Treats!" meaning the student who forgot to silence his or her phone can't come back to class without bringing homemade treats for the entire ensemble. Most students can't afford the time or money to break this rule. The other option is to work off the cell interruption by working in the music library. I love this rehearsal rule!

5) **High school students have an attention span of about eight minutes**. Younger students (and many adults) have even less. Switch activities every eight to ten minutes, even if it is only to stand and stretch or face a different direction.

6) **Change it up.** Students can stand or sit in different spots. Add decorations (balloons, new posters, crepe paper); sing while standing in circles; sing facing one another; sing according to hair color, sports team allegiance, or ice cream flavor preference. These variations help break up the rehearsal and still sneak in lots of repetition during the class period. The changes will help the choir focus and anticipate what will come next in the rehearsal.

7) **The director must be energized and leave personal problems at the door**. Attitudes are contagious.

8) **If a number or an activity is not working, throw in the towel and start over**. My good friend Heather, a fabulous graphic designer, drafts our Butler camp brochures each summer. After spending many months working on a Butler brochure, Heather decided it just wasn't working. She scrapped the design and started again from scratch. Her new design was truly magical, to match the camp theme that year. As educators, we need to be willing to start over when music or choreography doesn't work.

9) **Be efficient with the talents and time of band members, choreographers, and set designers.** If the people are not needed, don't make them sit through the rehearsal. Communicate the rehearsal plan.

10) **Unless you are bleeding**, **don't utter a sound**. In other words, students don't talk unless the director asks.

11) **Revive the rehearsal** with sectionals or an energy booster such as jumping jacks or an icebreaker game. Check out two of my resource books from Shawnee Press, *Icebreakers: 60 Fun Activities That Will Build a Better Choir* and *Icebreakers 2: 64 MORE Games and Fun Activities*. Teachers around the world have described these top-selling books as useful and effective in the classroom.

12) **Save questions until the end**. If it is that important, the student will not forget the problem and can wait to ask at the end of the class. It is imperative not to break the flow of the rehearsal. Normally, the student will forget or you will have solved the problem by the end of class.

13) **Start every rehearsal singing**. Save announcements for the end of class.

14) If students feel the need to "critique," **have them write it down** and turn it in to you after class.

15) **Make rehearsals fun.** Let students see the bigger picture (for example, videos, photos, e-mails, visits, and stories from alums). Students will enjoy rehearsals so much more when they understand why they are rehearsing.

16) **Use humor in rehearsals**. If you aren't funny or don't feel comfortable using humor in the classroom, take thirty seconds and show a YouTube clip or a quick PowerPoint presentation. Many of these excerpts are amusing and educational. Use this to transition from one activity to the next.

17) **Technology is your friend**. Ask your students for help. It seems the younger they are, the more they know. ☺ Use Twitter or Facebook to share your comments or post homework assignments. An application for Smart-phones called "Dance Formations" gives you access to 84 dance formations. For a few dollars you can get ideas for groups between 5-18 dancers/couples.

18) **If the rehearsal is to last one hour, make a lesson plan for an hour and a half.** Always be overprepared. Some ideas may not take as long. Time is precious.

> If the rehearsal is to last one hour, make a lesson plan for an hour and a half.

19) **Use an icebreaker** to get to know class members, break up the rehearsal procedure, or refocus students. (See item 11 for my shameless plug. I wouldn't be plugging the Icebreaker books if I didn't see such great results in my own classes and rehearsals. They really do work!)

20) **Use rehearsals to the max**. Avoid letting students mark through numbers. Marking sends the wrong message to the body/emotions/instincts about what it takes to perform. **Now, go REHEARSE!**

I'M JUST SAYING...

I like to think of planning a rehearsal the same way I plan or program a show. The opening activity should be similar to an opening number—catch the students' attention and make them want more. Is there a novelty number, a commercial break in the middle of class? Students need fresh ideas to remain attentive throughout the rehearsal. Are transitions smooth? Are you "edu-taining" your audience? There must be some meat for them to chew on—in class and onstage. How about a robust closing? Finish the rehearsal on a strong, positive note, leaving the singers wanting more. The finale or the final minutes need to leave the participants pumped up and excited for the next show/rehearsal.

And don't forget to applaud your students. The music classroom is one place we can show our appreciation for those around us.

CHAPTER 3:
CHOREOGRAPHY

SHALL WE DANCE?

The *King and I* was set in Bangkok in the 1860s, and to Anna (an early music educator), the King's invitation of "Shall we dance?" might have been a legitimate question. In the twenty-first century it is purely rhetorical. With the popularity of the dance reality shows and even the "dance wars" (two show choirs with unlimited budgets!), students are inundated with movement and music. Today, musicians realize that physical movement adds life to choral music, both in rehearsal and in performance. Movement and music are closely related, and the relationship provides synergy for everyone involved. This list will remind you the instructor, your students, the parents, and the administration about the importance of movement in the classroom.

Let us choose to *DANCE!*

WHY MOVEMENT AND DANCE ARE IMPORTANT IN THE CLASSROOM AND FOR THE STAGE

Students will...

- use both sides of the brain, thus faster learning will take place.
- cultivate creativity.
- retain lyrics for a longer period of time and memorize earlier.
- rehearse facial choreography, improving vocal sound.
- absorb basic stage directions and stage terminology.
- incorporate theater skills.
- learn proper stage etiquette.
- develop correct posture and proper body alignment.
- employ self-confidence skills.
- increase listening skills by combining movement and musical instructions.
- have an energetic sound.
- advance in working with peers, improving teamwork skills.
- give the audience more variety and entertainment in performances.
- interact professionally with the opposite sex.
- improve in overall coordination.
- practice eye-hand coordination.
- be trained to isolate the body.

- study foreign languages through use of French ballet terms, Italian music terms, and world dance vocabulary.
- increase musical awareness by pantomiming playing a musical instrument.
- work from the center of the body, using core muscles.
- have more flexibility as a performer—physically and mentally.
- utilize stage poise.
- gain a broader knowledge of history through world dance, cultural traditions, and ethnic costumes.
- better their understanding of backstage technical aspects such as lights, sound, and set.
- discover natural rhythms through counting and pulses in the music.
- exercise daily and work on physical fitness.
- better their basic motor skills.
- be successful in more than one venue.
- communicate with hearing-impaired audience members if performing in sign language.
- have fun on stage and in the classroom.
- learn life-long lessons.

May we be like Anna so that we can listen and learn from those around us. Help us not be stubborn like the King, who was stuck in tradition and self-absorption, but enjoy "getting to know" more about this musical adventure. In the end, it truly is about making the best of the journey and not just reaching the destination. Students will learn, grow, have fun, and continue to learn life lessons.

CREATING CHOREOGRAPHY

A close friend and colleague gave me an article on "the kitchen sink method" of creativity. I enjoy reading about creativity and agree that most artists and writers use some version of the kitchen sink method each time they create. In a nutshell, the kitchen sink method is doing a variety of things, for example, reading a paragraph from each of eight different books, then listening to four or five differing styles of music, and ending with physical activity. (I add a pedicure but that is my own ritual. Hey, don't knock it if it works. Where do you think I am writing this chapter right now? ☺)

After doing all the above, which may take an hour or so, go back to the music, think through the choreography you need to create, and bingo! Generally a light bulb will

> **If you believe in the work, so will your students.**

appear and then a spark of an idea. You are training your right brain to become more active by throwing everything—including the kitchen sink—into that creative right hemisphere. Too many times when faced with having to hurriedly produce choreography, we don't trust our own instincts and talents. If you are the choreographer or have artistic creative decisions before you, give yourself permission to be creative and don't second-guess yourself. If you believe in the work, so will your students. If you are passionate about your show, your students will be as well.

If someone else is planning to assist with the choreography, make sure you talk through general guidelines and agree on the philosophy.

TWENTY CHOREOGRAPHY GUIDELINES

1) Have **the material choreographed before the first rehearsal**. Choreographing on the spot wastes valuable time and energy. Have formations planned out in advance.

2) The show must **line up with your vision**. Music + Choreography = Director's Vision.

3) **Think levels**: bent knees, stools, risers, platforms, lifts, scaffolding, ladders, sitting in chairs, standing on chairs, sitting on the floor, sitting on risers, lying on the floor, partner lifts, etc.

4) Be sure the **choreography isn't so wild** it can't be tamed for cleaning.

5) **Gender identity—male vs. female**. Guys need to be guys on stage and girls should be feminine and curvy. Use stride position (wide second position) for girls only in hip-hop style and if they're dressed appropriately.

6) If **unison choreography—then be totally in unison**, perfectly together and clean.

7) **Pacing of the show**. Give the audience time to rest. Don't overdo ballad choreography.

8) **Unison vs. part choreography**. Use both in the show for variety.

9) **KISS principle**—Keep It Simple "Silly." More isn't always better in the dance world.

10) **Stay away from trite choreography**. An example to avoid is "but I love you…" (pointing to rear end, eye, heart, and partner). This is a melodramatic, over-the-top-silly style.

11) **Entrances, exits, and all transitions** (moving from place to place) should flow and be creative.

12) Pretend you are **working for MTV**, which films all parts of the body, not just the face.

13) **Think like a producer.** Think big. If you can dream it, you can achieve the dream.

14) Heinz 57 variations—**variety is the spice of life**. Think out of the box. Try not to repeat ideas.

15) **Choreograph in tempo**. Don't slow down the lyrics when actually choreographing.

16) To keep the number from looking busy, **choreograph phrases and not each word**.

17) After creating a single phrase, **immediately add it back in the section** and in entirety.

18) **Never repeat chorus a third time with same choreography.** Change formations and add layers the third repeat so it is fresh for the audience.

19) Choreography should be **eye-appealing and evenly weighted**. Symmetry on stage is not always required, but after a while, the performance will feel lopsided if one side of stage has more action and bodies than the other side of the stage. Use technology to search for public domain pictures and spacing ideas.

20) **Look at the age and talent level of the performers.** Challenge but don't frustrate the students.

TEACHING CHOREOGRAPHY

There is a belief that anyone can teach and that anyone can be a choreographer. Working with my own students, dance captains, student choreographers, and professionals, I've decided that being a teacher is a calling—a higher calling. Not everyone has the gift to be a teacher. And not everyone can teach dance. If you choose to use student choreographers or guest teachers, be sure the director observes the routine and the choreographer's teaching skills before the first practice.

CHOREOGRAPHERS—TAKE NOTE!

- Students learn **best what is taught first**. If a choreographer decides to change moves, formations, or even little details, the performers will resort back to what they learned first. With enough rehearsal, they can make those changes. It's easiest to teach it right the first time.

- Choreographers **do not have time to waste** when teaching. If the routine is in two parts, teach the dance captain before class and split the ensemble in half. The choir will learn twice as fast.

- **Use an authoritative but not authoritarian voice**. Be pleasant but firm.

- Save answering **questions for the end of a rehearsal**. Students normally want attention or to show off what they know. Ask the student to write down the comment or remember it until the end of class, when you can then discuss it. If it is important, they'll remember. If not, valuable class time was saved.

- Choreographers are teachers. They need to dress, speak, and **behave professionally**. Students will emulate what is in front of them. Teach and, when necessary, use words.

- **Use the text of the song** to help students memorize and learn the choreography faster. If it is a dance break, use counts when demonstrating.

- **Use terms that aren't above the performer's heads**. Say "bent knees" instead of plié; "slide" as a substitute for chassé; "kick a football and set" in place of Charleston. But if the group consists of dancers or music theater students, use actual dance terminology.

- **Be positive and excited about the material**. X = X. If you are excited about the new show, everyone will be excited. More about X = X later.

- **Assign partners**. Many students feel uncomfortable and nervous about not being chosen when instructed to "partner up." Instead, the director or choreographer should pair up individuals and place them in positions. If you need to save time with a big group, turn the exercise into a quick icebreaker game. "Find someone who has the same brand of shoes, or eye color, or birthday month. You have 15 seconds to find a partner, now go!"

- **Choose different faces for the front** row on each number. If the ensemble is competing and a dancer or dancers are needed in front, audition for those spots so everyone has a fair chance.

- **Don't stay in vertical lines**. The sound will get caught in the big hair of the girl in front. Use windows. Mama paid too much for the costume to not see it.

- **Have fun!**

I'M JUST SAYING...

Student choreographers must learn to be teachers—to be respectful, disciplined, and think creatively out of the box. As teachers, they must be flexible and learn to go with the flow. The students must prove to me that they are serious about the art before I let them "try and fly." I invite my student choreographer or dance captains to workshops and productions, and to attend other classes I teach, such as tap dancing, voice, show choir, and choreography. It is important for them to attend summer workshops. If they are willing to sacrifice time, energy, and money, I know they are on the right track. Once they've mastered the above, I am ready to recommend them as choreographers and give them my stamp of approval. There are some hoops to jump through, but the final product will be beneficial for all involved.

CLEANING CHOREOGRAPHY

As a twenty-five-year veteran adjudicator for the Keynote SHOWSTOPPERS™ show choir invitational, I had the fortune to see hundreds of amazing and outstanding show choirs at Walt Disney World and Disneyland. Ron Hellems, one of the "grandfathers of show choir" (sorry, Ron, but think of it as a title of respect), devised a score sheet that was novel for show choirs at the time. Instead of being responsible for everything in the show and on the score sheet—vocals, choral blend, balance between sections, the band, arrangements, choreography, special effects, selecting dance soloists, best stage crew, best soloists (male and female)—show choir judges were hired to evaluate one thing and one thing only. It was an expensive undertaking to bring in specialty judges from all over the country, but I applaud Keynote's innovative efforts to make an impact on the show choir world.

The judges used score sheets either for general effect (visual or music) or for ensemble effect (visual or music). The general-effect scores reflected the show's effectiveness and the ensemble scores rated the performers' accuracy. I loved both categories, but the visual ensemble effect was right up a dance teacher's alley. I'm just glad I was on the opposite side of the table from the competing choirs. It is easy to pass judgment while looking for uneven lines, unpointed toes, dropped hats, costume malfunctions, and spacing mishaps. Everyone loves to be a critic. I was always grateful that my own ensembles weren't being evaluated. The easy part is pointing out the mistakes, but how do you clean up choreography once it is taught?

TWENTY-FIVE IDEAS FOR A PERFECT "ENSEMBLE VISUAL" SCORE

1) **Revisit the teaching of the choreography**—teach slowly and accurately the first time. If choreography is taught precisely and methodically from day one, students will be aware of the correct position.

2) **Use mirrors** if at all possible. If your school doesn't have mirrors, find a facility that does (for example, a local dance studio, a gym, a large dressing room, or even a place with strong reflections from windows).

3) Bring in a **guest person for the day**. This could be another instructor, a dance teacher, or an alum: anyone with "new eyes." The students will hear comments with a new twist. Even though the person critiquing is probably saying things that have already been said, it will be with a fresh voice and expressed in a new way.

4) Be careful **not to include dissipation**—extra movements with each action. If arms are supposed to go from a low V to a high V, don't take the long way to get there. Don't complicate the moves, and do take the shortest means from one move to the next.

5) **Practice using props immediately**. Props add a lot visually but take up rehearsal time. Never add props the week (or day!) of a show, no matter how much you trust your ensemble.

6) Use **colored tape or a number line** on the floor. This will save time in rehearsal. Be aware of spatial relationships—students need to be in windows or correct formations.

7) Rehearse **with mirrors and then turn away**. Mirrors may be used as a crutch, so balance time spent with and without them.

8) **Split the group in half**. Let one half perform while the other half writes critiques on paper. Ask for positive comments as well as criticism. Then switch groups.

9) **Make a rehearsal video.** Students will improve quickly when they see for themselves what needs to be fixed. Put the video on Dropbox (*dropbox.com*) or e-mail to each individual so he or she can observe the rehearsal and write a critique before the next class period or rehearsal.

10) **Teach recovery**. If a hat or another prop falls on the floor, don't pretend it didn't happen. Pick it up when the music and choreography allow. Until you do so, the audience will focus only on that hat on the ground.

11) **Shoelaces to the audience**. Where your feet are, there your body will follow.

12) The **audience should see and not hear entrances and exits**. Stay on your toes while moving.

13) Teach students **not to anticipate movements**. Dance captains often move early as they are used to "helping" the ensemble remember what comes next in the routine.

14) **Spot when turning**. This is a dance concept and means that the person spinning needs to stare at an eye-level spot (i.e., the clock on the back wall). The spinner keeps staring at the spot as long as possible. This helps the face stay front, allowing the audience to see the performer. Most important, it means no dizzy spells and better vocals.

15) Singers should **walk naturally** and not try to walk to the beat. Unless the music specifically calls for a choreographed walk, the tempo shouldn't control you, or movement will look and feel awkward.

16) Students **must feel comfortable** with the choreography and staging. If they feel uncomfortable, so will the audience. See **X = X** on page **102**.

17) **Simplify choreography** if needed. Each student needs to feel good about his or her performance.

18) "**Never mark!** Go full out." ~ Rachelle Rak, Fosse dancer who appeared in the 2008 Broadway documentary *Every Little Step*.

19) Give **hands specific positions**, or you'll have "spaghetti arms" ending up all over the place.

20) **Repetition is the key**. Rehearse over and over until it is second nature.

21) **Know the choreography** but also be able to perform. Use facial expressions to communicate the message.

22) Choreography can be the same, but **personality** is what gives the group its own flair and style.

23) Maximize your impact! **Teach transfer of knowledge**. Remember all that was taught and bring it to the next rehearsal.

24) "Choreographers and teachers should **look above the performers' heads** to see who is not catching on," says Adam Parson, Blue Power Ranger and LA Edge Dance instructor.

25) **"Perfect practice makes perfect performance."** ~ Valerie Lippoldt Mack.

> "Perfect practice makes perfect performance."
> ~ Valerie Lippoldt Mack.

Speaking of cleaning choreography, it is a good idea to keep a bottle of hand sanitizer by the door. Performers can use it as they enter and exit the rehearsal room. Large bottles are available at wholesale stores. It is worth the expense.

I'M JUST SAYING...

One of my favorite choreography stories took place early in my career. A high school had asked me to choreograph the musical George M! *based on the life of George M. Cohan. The lead who was selected had never danced, much less tap danced, and it was my job to get him ready in four weeks of rehearsal. This young man, "Joe," was not coordinated, to say the least, and was a quiet, unassuming person—definitely not a member of the "in" crowd.*

The two of us worked endless hours, but the dancing wasn't getting any better. Opening night finally came, and in the middle of the big solo tap number, Joe got his arm stuck in his vest. The orchestra paused and you could have heard a pin drop. He struggled for what seemed like an eternity. Finally, realizing the costume change wasn't going to work, he ripped the vest in half, threw it on the floor, stepped to the edge of the stage and started tapping as I had never seen him tap. The crowd went wild and gave him a standing ovation in the middle of the number.

That night, Joe became "George M." It didn't matter how clean the tap number was or wasn't. I'll never forget that moment—nor will Joe. It was a life-changing moment for us both! Years afterward, Joe, now "Dr. Joe," told his parents that being onstage in his high school musical was the best foundation for his later life. I treasure the thank-you note he wrote and refer to it often.

WORKING WITH CHOREOGRAPHERS

If you plan on hiring a student or a professional to teach choreography to your ensemble, be sure to discuss everything long before the first rehearsal. It could save the director, the instrumentalists, the cast, AND the choreographer from tearing their hair out. Most importantly, it assures the entire team of having the best experience possible.

The biggest problem associated with hiring and working with a choreographer is … LACK OF COMMUNICATION! It is frustrating being at either end—I know, as I've been on both sides. It is

easy to get so wrapped up in all the show details that the director forgets that his or her decisions affect many. Here are some words of advice I've collected over the years—most recently from some of my kids venturing out into the field of choreography.

A STEP-BY-STEP GUIDE FOR WORKING WITH CHOREOGRAPHERS

1) Discuss a contract before the first rehearsal.

2) Stick with the contract. Don't add seven more rehearsals the week of the show and then expect the choreographer to attend each and every last-minute rehearsal.

3) Figure in gas mileage and expenses when deciding on an honorarium.

4) If the choreographer is on the artistic team, let the choreographer take part in some of the decisions. Do invite him or her to sit on the audition panel and then ask for (and follow) the input at the end of the auditions.

5) Give all cuts to the choreographer at the beginning with sheet music and a CD. Don't expect him or her to find a piano and play the orchestra reduction. Please don't suggest finding it on YouTube. Suggestions are great, but the choreographers need the same tools that the director has.

6) Give plenty of notice and enough time to prepare before a rehearsal. If you want brilliant choreography, give ample time for the creation. If you don't care, some choreographers can choreograph on the spot. I don't recommend this as most directors work on a tight time budget. Creating on the spot is sometimes confusing for the participants and doesn't always work.

7) Clearly state the ensemble's talent level. If most of the students are signed up for advanced dance classes, be sure to include that information. If this is the first show choir at the school, inform the choreographer of that, as well.

8) Give an accurate account of numbers. To make formations, the choreographer needs to specify the exact amounts of guys, girls, and soloists. Give notice of any number changes before rehearsals begin. Advise choreographers of other conditions that could affect the safety of a student and/or staging, such as wheelchairs, crutches, visual impairments, and other physical conditions. Students with these special conditions need to be blocked in the routine, but it is helpful for the choreographer to have advance notice for each situation.

9) Treat the choreographer as a special guest. Teach students to be respectful, as the choreographer is there for their benefit—to make them look better. The choreographer shouldn't have to spend time disciplining the ensemble. It helps if the director remains in the room and takes notes. This will save time later and keeps students in line and focused.

10) Don't allow students to ask any questions until the end of the rehearsal. Those queries interrupt the flow. Instead, have the students try to imitate the choreographer's style and exact moves. Have them watch for details.

11) Check with the instrumentalists to make sure performance tempos are the tempos the choreographer is expecting. Certain numbers can be dangerous if performed too fast or too slow.

12) Give guidelines before the choreographer teaches a routine, not during a teaching session. If lifts, partner dancing, or hip rolls are banned, be sure this is mentioned before the choreographer invests time originating material.

13) If the director feels a part of the routine is not working, discuss this in private and not in front of students.

14) Be sure to insist on outside dance rehearsals. If students don't retain the dance moves and the same routines are being repeated each rehearsal, it is a waste of everyone's time. Transfer the knowledge from one day to the next.

15) Students should come dressed to rehearse: proper dance shoes, dance attire, and no hats.

16) Explain the guidelines of using student choreographers and assistants.

17) Talk face to face with your choreographer. Maintain a professional relationship.

18) Give credit to your choreographer(s). If you don't have a printed program, announce from the stage.

19) Treat the choreographer professionally onstage and off. Talk positively about the individual and his or her work.

20) Meet after the performance(s) and have a wrap-up meeting. Make note of how to improve in the future.

I'M JUST SAYING...

I was lucky enough to have "show choir angels" such as Doug Anderson, Kirby Shaw, and Stevie Rivers watching over me when I first started in this business we call show choir. I remember the first time I adjudicated a show choir competition: I was in my early twenties and thought I had all the answers. I was hurriedly filling out the critique sheet and just knew that some lucky choral group would read my lofty advice and that it would suddenly rock their world.

A show choir "legend/angel" was also on the panel. That person came over and stood beside me, glancing at some of my scribbling. My angel advised that in the future I should bring a dictionary with me, as I had misspelled a word in the haste of spewing out my wisdom. The angel further reminded me about the professionalism of the business and that I should never be in so much of a hurry that I couldn't do things "right." And the angel suggested that in the future I might bring a calculator with me so I wouldn't be crunching numbers into the next group's set.

Another bit of advice I received that first time out was to order room service in the morning. The extra thirty minutes of sleep and a good breakfast would make all the difference in a long day of presenting workshops and being alert during the late-night competition. I follow that bit of advice to this day.

And a third bit of advice? Call home and say good night, each and every night—no matter what! Tell your family that you love them—even if you are traveling or getting home late. One can be so engrossed in work and/or be on the road that, unintentionally, family members and those you love are taken for granted. These are the people who deserve our best (not our leftover time and energy)! This is a constant battle for me, I will confess. I continually work on that "balance" issue every day. But no matter what, make time for family—FIRST!

P.S. Extra hugs and kisses to the Mack and Lippoldt families!

DANCING WITH STYLE

Have you ever felt that many of your show choir numbers looked similar? That even songs from different eras appear identical? That is why I created the "Dancing with Style" seminars. I have presented this workshop over the years and it has proved to be very helpful to music educators and students alike. Learn eight basic steps and turn them into a 64-count routine. Next, provide a few historical references and adjectives concerning various styles for the students to consider as they perform the 64-count basic routine in a variety of styles. This is not scientific or from any particular source but has proved to be fun and educational. You and your students will dance with style in no time at all.

---

8 "BASIC STEPS" ROUTINE:

8 counts.	8 walks in place (R, L, R, L, R, L, R, L)
8 counts.	4 step touch—half-time walks (Step R and touch L, Step L and touch R, repeat)
8 counts.	3-step turn (R, L, R and touch L; repeat to the left)
8 counts.	8 twists in place (twist down and up)
8 counts.	4 step kicks (R step-kick L, L step-kick R); repeat R and L
8 counts.	2 pivots (front to back and back to front)
8 counts.	4 jumps or hops in place
8 counts.	Slide to a pose and hold!

DECADES OF DANCE

In the following list, each time period includes some words or phrases to describe the time, actual dance steps, and, for the later time periods, a movie or musical depicting the era's dance styles. The shows were not necessarily filmed or produced during that time frame but portray the historical time period.

1400s-1600s. Renaissance; rebirth of humanism and revival of cultural achievement; new printing methods; clavichord and virginal invented. **Minuet, Mazurka, Contre Dance (French Square**

Dance), Sarabande, Morris Dancing.

1600s-1750s. Baroque period; dance closely linked to music, theater, and opera. Court dancing, especially **Minuet**. Composers: Bach (German), Handel (English), Vivaldi (Italian). The **English Country Dance** (in duple time) later developed into the **Cotillion** and the **Reel**. Baroque music suites had dance movements such as **Galliard, Courante, Gigue,** and **Allemande**. In Spain, **Flamenco dance**.

1750s-1850s. Classical period; Social upheaval, contrast of moods, simple melodies. Composers: Haydn, Mozart, Beethoven. Movie: *Amadeus*. **Round dance** culminated in the **Waltz**. Development of **Irish step dancing** from French and English dances. Invention of **Bolero**, a Spanish dance (although it did not become popular in the United States until the 1930s). **Appalachian folk dancing, Great Quadrille, Schottische,** and the elegant ballroom **Viennese Waltz.**

1820s-1900. Romantic period; Individuality, nationalism, exoticism, expanded range, pushing the envelope. Composers: Tchaikovsky, Wagner, Schubert. Movies: *Becoming Jane, Pride and Prejudice.* **Minuet**, various types of **round dance, Landler, Polonaise, Grand March, Virginia Reel, Two-Step,** the "**German**" **Dance**, the **Schottische**, Vienna Waltz (fast), **slow waltz.**

1880s-1920s. Vaudeville; big, overdone movements; trite and cheesy moves. Eddie Cantor, Burns and Allen, Charlie Chaplin, Will Rogers, Mae West, Nicholas Brothers, *If You Knew Susie, Oh You Beautiful Doll, Me and My Gal.* **American Indian Ghost Dance, Round Dancing, Old Virginia, Cotillion Walk, Two-Step.**

1900s. Turn of the century; new-fangled inventions, conservative clothing and hair; silent films, Berlin, Cohan and Ziegfeld. *Ragtime, Newsies, and Little Johnny Jones.* **Ragtime dances: Grizzly Bear, Turkey Trot, One-Step, Castle Walk, Cake Walk, Bunny Hug, Dip, Samba.**

1920s. Roaring '20s, flappers, sheiks, bobbed hair, lots of money, big and tight arm movements, *Thoroughly Modern Millie, Drowsy Chaperone,* and *Boyfriend.* Barbershop music and speakeasy. **Charleston, Black Bottom, Camel Walk, Varsity Drag, Shimmy, Fox Trot, Tango, Sugar Foot, Snake.**

1930s. Great Depression, slouching shoulders and a shot of novocaine in wrists, Shirley Temple, Fred and Ginger, Busby Berkeley, *Puttin' on the Ritz, Me and My Gal, Anything Goes, Top Hat.* **Jitterbug, Lindy, Swing, Big Apple, Little Apple, Conga, Shorty George, Truckin', Lindy Hop, Rumba, Mambo, Cha Cha, SusieQ, Lambeth Walk.**

1940s. Military, swing, bent knees and bottoms out, World War II, Hokey Pokey, *Meet Me in St. Louis, Holiday Inn, On the Town, Easter Parade.* **West Coast Swing, Boogie Woogie, Jive, Balboa, Carolina Shag, Shim Sham, Sugar Foot.**

1950s. Rock 'n' roll, bop, hand jive, poodle skirts, cleaner moves than what would come in the '60s, *Grease, Band Wagon, Jailhouse Rock, Rock Around the Clock, All Shook Up* and other Elvis movies. **Rock 'n' Roll, Stroll, Madison, Hand Jive, Bunny Hop, Conga, Swing, Cha-Cha, Bossa Nova, Bunny Hop.**

1960s. British invasion. The Beatles, war, protest rock, peace, flower power, hippies, psychedelic, loose ribcage, pelvic thrusts, John F. Kennedy, Vietnam, *Laugh-In,* sock hops, *Austin Powers, Hair, Bye Bye Birdie.* **Twist, Jerk, Monkey, Pony, Swim, Mashed Potato, Skate, Hitchhike, Egyptian, Temptation Walk, Locomotion, Shimmy, Funky Chicken, Monster Mash, Frug, Watusi, The Shake, Fish.**

1970s. Disco, line dances, dance used as a way for working class to escape from everyday routines, John Travolta's white leisure suit, platform shoes, mirror ball, Afros, bellbottom pants, Bee Gees, *Brady Bunch*, Abba's "Dancing Queen," *Saturday Night Fever, Stayin' Alive, A Chorus Line, Rocky.* **Hustle, Bus Stop, The Bump, Latin Hustle, Four Corners, Saturday Night Fever Line Dance, Disco Points, Time Warp, YMCA, Robot, Slam Dancing, Wackin'.**

1980s. "Me" generation. Punk rock, pop 'n' lock, country, Barry Manilow, Michael Jackson and "Thriller," big hair, MC Hammer and parachute pants, shoulder pads, leg warmers, break dancing, "Safety Dance," Ronald Reagan, *Footloose, Flashdance, Fame, Dirty Dancing, Tootsie, E.T., Urban Cowboy, You Got Served.* **Running Man, Moonwalk, The Electric Slide, Break Dancing, Pac-Man, Country Line Dancing, Walk Like an Egyptian, RoboCop, New Kids on the Block Moves, Funky Twist, Cabbage Patch, Roger Rabbit, Poppin', Wavin', Tickin'.**
1990s. Boy bands, rap, techno, hip-hop, Madonna, Vanilla Ice, bubble gum pop, Britney Spears, Paula Abdul, Janet Jackson, N'Sync, Disney movies, *Rent, Men In Black, Ghost.* **Country Two-Step, East Coast Swing, Salsa, Vogue, Macarena, Worm, Lambada, Achy Breaky Heart, Cha-Cha Slide, Cotton-Eyed Joe, The Grind, Crip Walk, Carlton Dance.**

2000s. Too soon to tell! Copying older dance styles, *Glee, In the Heights, SYTYCD, Step Up,* and Disney's *High School Musicals 1, 2, 3.* **The One-Two Step, Single Ladies, C-Walking, Krumping, Stanky Leg, Soulja Boy, Cupid Shuffle, Lady GaGa's Bad Romance, Cha-Cha Slide, Shoulder Lean, The Rockaway.**

DIVERSE DANCE STYLES AND GENRES

While some dance steps seem to belong to a certain time, other dance moves are not necessarily connected with a time period but evoke various feelings and images, or create visual effects. Here are a few:

Choralography. Simplified choreography or riser choreography. Great for large groups. Feet not involved. Stevie Rivers, John Jacobson, and Sally Albrecht are masters at choralography and have material available.

Gospel. Heartfelt, real, claps but no snaps, SAB voicing, robes, chest voice sound; spiritual, Jester Hairston, Dr. Rollo Dilworth, Albert McNeil and the Jubilee Singers, Dr. Andre Thomas, and Mark Hayes (arrangements).

Patriotic. Pride, lines, kicks, pinwheels, march, high knees, hand to heart, straight lines, national pride, a little more light-hearted than military style, *George M. Cohan.*

Military. Salute, more serious, clean moves, lines, marching, American flag, military personnel, uniform, honor the armed forces—all branches of military, *White Christmas, Gold Diggers of 1936.*

Country. Heels, toes, turned-out knees, cowboy hats, classic country, ride a horse, lasso, bandannas, cowboy boots, scuff heels, country line dances, *Big River, Will Rogers, Seven Brides for Seven Brothers, Annie Get Your Gun.*

Hillbilly. Goofy, blacked-out teeth, hambone (body percussion), sillier than country style, *Li'l Abner, Sadie Hawkins Day, Amoozin "But Confoozin', Beverly Hillbillies.*

Swing. Jitterbug/Lindy—East Coast and West Coast swing, rock step, partner lifts, Madding throw, straddle throw, kick and land in splits, *Stompin' at the Savoy, Swing Kids, Swing!*

Latin. Salsa, samba, cha-cha, rumba, tango, bossa nova, Latin-stance, hips, macho guys, sexy, Latin eyes, fancy footwork, red and black colors, Cuban Pete, *Strictly Ballroom, Mad Hot Ballroom, Shall We Dance?, In the Heights, Dirty Dancing.*

Ballroom. Stylistic, various styles, partner dancing, carriage upper lift, waltz, two step, foxtrot, tango, mambo, *So You Think You Can Dance, Dancing with the Stars, Strictly Ballroom, Burn the Floor.*

Soft Shoe. Light, sand, Fred Astaire, "Tea for Two" rhythm, slap legs, pull lamp shade, shuffles, soft-shoe step, step brush, Fred and Ginger, Tommy Tune, pretty as a picture, "Once in Love with Amy," "Nothing Could Be Finer Than to Be in Carolina," "Harrigan (H,A,double-R,I,G,A,N)."

Irish. Hard shoe, leap, line of serious dancers, arms to sides of body, hard tap shoes, green and black costumes, fast and furious feet, Michael Flatley, *River Dance, Lord of the Dance, Celtic Women.*

Broadway. Classic style, time steps, lines, kicks, top hats and canes, white gloves, showy numbers, weight shift (R and L) with hands on a table. *42nd Street, Curtains, A Chorus Line.*

11:00 Number. Big closing production number at the end of the show; for example, "For Good" from *Wicked*, "Betrayed" from *The Producers*, "You Can't Stop the Beat" from *Hairspray*, "Brotherhood of Man" from *How to Succeed in Business Without Really Trying.*

Jazz (Vocal). Snaps but few claps; scatting and improvisation, not choreographed, unique individuals, black outfits. Steve Zegree, Darmon Meader, Dave Cross, Kirk Macy, Deke Sharon, Michele Weir, Phil Matson, and Paris Rutherford are a few of the vocal jazz arrangers. Kirby Shaw, Roger Emerson, Mac Huff, Mark Brymer, Russ Robinson, and Greg Gilpin have more accessible arrangements for younger voices. *The Jazz Singer, De-Lovely.*

Fosse. Bowler hats, feet turned in, twisted postures, serious + humor, sultry, finger rolls, Fosse walks—leading with pelvic, banana jump, not always perfectly clean, not assigned gender, *Fosse, Sweet Charity, Chicago, Cabaret, Pippin, Pajama Game, All That Jazz* (the movie).

Novelty. Out of the box. Funny, ridiculous, edgy, abnormal, out of the box, edgy, not an opening or closing type number. The following musicals contain many novelty numbers: *Shrek, Spamalot, Xanadu, The Lion King, Avenue Q, Cats,* and *Wicked.*

Modern. Floor work, conceptual, individual, angry story line, filled with angst, self-absorbed. Audience is not always involved emotionally, but the dancers always are.

Liturgical. Sacred dancing, lots of symbolism, white robes, worship-style, streamers, Christian influence.

Sign Language. Communicating with hearing-impaired through hand symbols and letters to fit words and thoughts. ASL (American Sign Language) is more conceptual. SEE (Signing Exact English) is movement per word.

Funk. Low to the ground, sit, plié, lots of drum, more fists than jazz hands, masculine style of dance.

Punk. Circa 1975. Appears chaotic, slam dancing, jumping, punk clothes, almost cultish; makes a statement. The Ramones, The Bangles.

Hip-Hop. Danced to popular music, very rhythmic, improvisation, cleaner than street dancing.

Street. Like hip-hop but done with more of a rough edge, more intimidating attitude.

Break Dance. Head spins, floor work, dangerous if not trained, physical, tricks, poses, *Breakin', Beat Street, Flashdance, Wild Style, Breakin' 2* and *Electric Boogaloo.*

Pop 'n' Lock. Pop shoulders, isolation, lots of upper body, stiff arms, chain reaction of stiffening and loosening muscles, lighter attitude than Krump style of dance. Michael Jackson's *This is it.*

Krump. Similar to Pop 'n' Lock, jerky, not a happy dance. A type of street dance characterized by free, expressive, exaggerated, and highly energetic movement involving arm swings, chest pops, and stomps. *Bring It On: All or Nothing.*

Bollywood. The term comes from combining Bombay with Hollywood. Indian film music, melodramatic Busby Berkeley-style musical production number performed with a large Indian cast; peacock fingers, *Slum Dog Millionaire, Bombay Dreams, Shakalaka Boom Boom,* and *Moulin Rouge.*

Eclectic. Meshing various styles in a show or in a number. "Simply Irresistible" in the musical *Contact; Moulin Rouge*; the vocal pop style in *Scarlet Pimpernel*, a musical set in late 1700s; *Joseph and the Amazing Technicolor Dreamcoat.*

I'M JUST SAYING...

The vocal and dance styles must match. Use choreography that is authentic and stylistic. Musicians wouldn't think about performing a fourteenth-century madrigal with a rock and roll interpretation. Ridiculous, you say, and yet many times this is what happens when choreography is added. Why would this piece of the art be any different? Let these simple ideas be inspiring. Your students will soon be singing and dancing in style.

> The vocal and dance styles must match. Use choreography that is authentic and stylistic.

STAGE PRESENCE

I have a game I like to play when invited to adjudicate an event. Whether it's a show choir competition, dance team audition, cheerleading tryout, Miss America scholarship pageant, barbershop contest, or even a solo audition with my own students, my record is amazingly accurate. Now that I've started sharing my "secrets of the trade" at various workshops, I admit that the stakes are getting higher. Do I have your attention yet? OK, here's the gist of the game.

As the performer(s) enter and/or warm up before the event, I observe the level of confidence, posture, stage attitude, and professionalism *off*stage. I also see how the accompanist and stagehands are treated—all before the performer sings or says anything. I quickly jot a ranking on a separate piece of paper and tuck it away in my briefcase. With the hectic nature of the competition schedule, I usually completely forget about the paper with the rankings until I'm on the plane or in the car the next day. Surprisingly, I have about a 95% accuracy rate in placing the groups or the individuals in the right order and choosing the winning group. Again, this is *before* the performance begins!

How, you ask, is that possible? I've included some things I look for as I "play" the game and study the preshow. Stage presence begins offstage and carries through the entire performance. Students must have confidence and yet not become cocky or conceited.

BODY LANGUAGE—"SHOW CHOIR RULES!" ONSTAGE AND OFF

- **Stage presence shouldn't be hindered by weak posture**. Body posture is important. Keep the spine straight! There are lots of tricks for teaching posture. Standing with your back to the door and keeping shoulders touching the door frame is one of the easiest.

- The **first impression is like a firm handshake**. Own it and be confident. You never get a second chance to make a first impression.

- **Move on purpose**. Be cautious not to pace back and forth. Feet have a purpose—no casual feet.

- **When standing, look alive. When sitting, sit as if standing.**

- **No pickin' or scratchin'** at any time. (Sorry! My Kansas roots keep coming through!)

- An **organized entrance articulates discipline** and impresses the audience (and judges).

- **Avoid unnecessary moving**, talking, or any excessive actions that draw unnecessary attention.

- **Let your face shine**. Don't let the costume or choreography upstage your face.

- **Be convincing on stage**. We'll see the clock if *you* do. Make us believe.

- **Remain animated**. Watch out for energy roller coasters; blend in with the rest of the ensemble.

- **Make eye contact with the audience** when entering the room.

- **Commit to the fact that you are good**. Do everything 150 percent. Engage your entire body.

- **Sing to one person** at a time.

- **Clean is fantastic but personality is most important.**

- **Think before you speak.** Choose words carefully and have a plan before going on stage.

- You need to **be different to stand out**. Judges look for the "it" or the magic in the performer.

- **"Perfect practice makes perfect performance!"** and "**Practice makes permanent.**"
  ~ Mrs. Mack

I'M JUST SAYING...

Rachelle Rak, Fosse dancer and Broadway performer, shared her tips on success: Never walk out of the house without putting on makeup and heels, as you are always presenting yourself. And never give less than 100 percent. Good performers never mark. There is a fine line between being "found" and being "found out."

PROGRAMMING

Important elements in the success of a performance include the selection of the repertoire and the order of the program. Programming will change depending on location of the show, the audience, requested length of show, stage space, and desired educational value. Will your selected program transport the audience to another place? My goal is twofold: letting the audience experience a range of emotions and sending them out whistling a show tune.

Show choir should be a happy art. The news is filled with tragedy and sadness and, unfortunately, those will still be around when students walk out of your music class. Your students could benefit from cheerful sentiments found in many pieces of music. Let them escape into the world of music—even if for an hour a day. Above all, keep the audience on their toes. Add surprise and magic for a positively entertaining and memorable experience for all performers and audience.

There are many avenues in which you can showcase your members—as a whole or individually. Feature the choir's combo or spotlight a special talent in the group—a student who can clog, yodel, juggle, twirl a baton, skate, or "trick." How about highlighting a young musician who possesses a gift in composition? Take a talent survey at the beginning of the school year, as oftentimes the most talented students are also your most humble ones. Remember, if you have to tell someone how great you are, you probably aren't! (Just a little hint for first-year teachers who might not have learned this yet.) This adage applies to students, their parents, and other faculty members. ☺

Repertoire choices can make or break the show. Look for variety in styles, tempos, lyrics, and challenges. Allow students to recommend a number for the director's consideration. This exercise gives the students some ownership in the program. Explain to the ensemble how difficult programming truly is: It is not just selecting a favorite song, but rather making all the pieces of the puzzle fit in neatly and nicely so the show has a flow. Break down any walls between the audience and the show choir with the literature.

FORMULA FOR A "PACKAGE" SHOW

1) **Opener:** Must be "we're happy to be here" and up-tempo, and must set the theme of the show. Show the audience that you can handle the "choir" part of show choir. Grab their attention!

2) **Second Number**: Could be a swing number, or slower in tempo than the opener. But keep the show moving forward.

3) **Ballad**: Challenge the ensemble with a performance of an *a cappella* number. Make sure the text speaks to the ensemble. The audience needs a visual break. Stage the ballad, but don't overdo movement.

4) **Novelty Number**: Something fun and crazy. A novelty number must be over the top or the audience will not understand. Never start with a novelty number—the audience won't have a sense of "normalcy" and will be confused. Comedy is good, but the audience needs to know without a doubt that the comedy is on purpose. Remember stage manners and don't poke fun at anyone.

5) **Featured Variety Number**: Solo or small ensemble (trio or quartet). Use time for costume change.

6) **Up-Tempo Number**: Fun and leads right into the last number.

7) **Closer:** Best number in the show. Opening number is second best. Grab the audience and build right up to the climax of the final number. Leave the audience wanting more—not less!

8) **Bow:** Must explode and be bigger than the last note of the closing number.

9) **Encore**: Something really short and sweet. Acknowledge applause and say, "THANK YOU!"

I'M JUST SAYING...

Don't be afraid to get away from the usual "package" show. If your ensemble has opened with "Another Op'nin', Another Show" for twenty consecutive years, then it is time to mix it up. Be brave and daring (but not stupid!). If you believe in the show's concept and promise, so will they.

True entertainment is about winning over the audience. If you want to keep the audience returning show after show, be mindful in your planning. Mr. Rhee Gold, a wise dance teacher and a pioneer in the dance education field, trains teachers to program with the "dad" (or a convention of truck drivers) in mind. Will a dad be happy sitting through a three-hour production? Will a dad be happy listening to a show and not hearing one word sung in his native language? What if the choreography is so involved that the diction is lost? Don't subject your audiences to this type of agony. Furthermore, many of the dads not only are supportive by attending but also are footing the bill for the fundraisers that didn't go as planned (candy bars, trash bags, eggs, car washes, etc.), paying for costumes, driving the student to and from extra rehearsals, filling up the gas tank, working an extra job to help pay for extracurricular activity fees, and so forth. Those dads totally deserve a well-thought-out program.

SUCCESSFUL PROGRAMMING TIPS: (NOT JUST FOR DADS!)

- **Choose a wider repertoire** that will appeal to a cross section of people.

- **Facilitate the flow of the show** with a theme or an overall idea.

- **Transitions can really help the flow of the show**. Use music to segue from number to number, every time. Silence can be very awkward on stage.

- **Use the element of surprise**. Will little Johnny pick and flick? If you've ever watched a program of kindergartners on stage, you will understand and appreciate that statement.

- **Bookend a show**. Start with a musical idea and come back to it in the finale.

- If your group is capable, throw in an *a cappella* **number** or one with different instruments. Get away from using the piano on every selection.

- **Celebrate traditions**. If your school has sung "Edelweiss" at the end of every concert and it is a school tradition, don't alter immediately. Sometimes change is needed and other times traditions are good. Don't question or modify the hallowed tradition if it is an annual ritual.

- **Save your "money moves" for the end**. Don't give it all away at the beginning.

- If you perform a poignant and/or moving number, give the audience **time to collect their emotions**. One suggestion would be to have the pianist play a reprise of the number.

- **Magic is a must**. If using an emcee, ask him or her not to interrupt the show and announce each number. Keep introductions short, mix them up, and don't do all from the stage. Keep the audience guessing. If you have a printed program, a phrase such as "numbers will be selected from the following…" is a nice way to build suspense throughout the event.

- **Vary the size of the performing ensemble**. Add solos, duets, quartets, emcees.

- **Vary the placement of ensembles**. Relocate in the performance space, not always in front.

- **Sing in surround sound**. This can be especially fun during the holiday season with candles, hand bells, or glow sticks.

I'M JUST SAYING…

Fred Waring used to tell about his first job at a local bakery. He had to be at work each morning by 4 a.m., and Fred's task was to catch the hot loaves of bread and pass them to the next person in line. At that time of morning, the rhythmic, repetitive tossing and catching of the loaves lulled the young workers to sleep, and many would start to doze on the job. To keep them alert, the baker would pause every now and then before tossing a loaf, creating a break in the steady rhythm. This syncopation in the tossing rhythm kept young Fred and the other workers on their toes. Mr. Waring remembered that important lesson as he began his career in programming TV shows. Keep your audience alert by changing the pace of the show and keeping the surprise factor alive.

THEME AND VARIATIONS

Audiences enjoy following a loosely-put-together story line or theme when attending shows. Songs that are grouped together make it easier for patrons to stay attuned and interested. However, if a theme gets too restricted, the idea could backfire. The audience will spend time guessing what piece will be next or how a certain number does or doesn't fit into the theme.

A helpful icebreaker to use in your classroom is from the resource book ***Icebreakers: 60 Fun Activities That Will Build A Better Choir***! The game "Musical Categories" on page 13 is a fun way for students to brainstorm ideas for your ensemble or program. Throw out a musical theme and ask the students to come up with song titles for your next performance.

One of the best resources for finding song ideas is included in *The GREEN BOOK of Songs by Subject: The Thematic Guide to Popular Music* by Jeff Green. This reference book works like a dictionary: You look up keywords (perhaps topics you are teaching) and the book lists titles, artists, and record label information for songs related to that topic. The book has more than 35,000 song references by more than 9,100 artists. There are nearly 1,800 key word categories across more than 1,500 pages. An online version of the book is available for a monthly fee.

THEME AND VARIATION IDEAS FOR ALL YOUR CHORAL ENSEMBLES

SPECIALTY THEMES

Advance in Dance

Anything Goes!

Art in Motion

Art Is Calling

Blood, Sweat, and Jazz Hands

British Invasion (The Beatles, Rolling Stones, Paul Revere & The Raiders, Spice Girls)

(The) Circus of Life

Dance Evolution

Dancin' Through the Decades

Decades of Dance

Disney Magic

Duets (famous couples)

Everything Old Is New Again

Giving of the Greens

Glee-tastic

Goin' Green

Happily Ever After …

Heroes: Teachers, Military, Parents, the American Work Force

It's All Relative (We Are Family, Brotherhood of Man, Sisters, Your Mama Don't Dance, Neighbor's Chorus)

It's a Jungle Out There (Lion Sleeps Tonight, Welcome to the Jungle, Tarzan, *Jungle Book*)

It's an Art

It's in the TEXT! (play on words—cell texting/lyrics)

It Takes Two (male and female, other pairs)

Just Du-et (like Nike slogan)

Let Me Take You on a Sea Cruise

Let's Go to the Movies!

Live to Dance and Sing!

Magical Years of Ears

Musical Memoirs

(A) New Attitude

(A) Night at the Movies

Night of the Living Zoo (animals theme)

Nights of Glee

(The) Oz Trilogy or Follow the Yellow Brick Road Home (*The Wizard of Oz*, *The Wiz*, *Wicked*)

Peace, Love, and Glee!

Rock Band (songs from the popular Rock Band video games)

Rock and Roll Is Here to Stay

Salute to America

Screen to Stage (Hollywood to Broadway)

Sea Cruise (ocean creatures, destinations, vacations)

Show Choir Forecast (storms, weather)

(The) Silver Screen

Sing a Rainbow

Sing for the Green

Song Sung Blue (colors)

Speed Limit '65 (songs from the '60s)

Stax of Wax (songs from the '50s)

Thanks for the Memories

Under the Big Top

Under the Sea

Villains and Heroes (good vs. evil)

Wild West

Zoo-bilee! (zoo animals)

WORLD AND DESTINATION THEMES

A New World

Around the World in Eighty Songs

Buckle Up!

City Lights

Compassing World Music
(The) Cosmosphere
Destination ... Showtime!
(The) Final Frontier
Find Your WAY
From the Big Apple (start with New York-themed songs)
Get into My Car! (travel)
God Bless America
(The) Golden Age of Broadway
(GPS)—Go the Distance Singing
Great White Way (Broadway)
It's a Capital Idea
It's a Wonderful World
I've Been Everywhere!
(The) Journey
Livin' in America (occupations)
Music Around the World
Music Makes the World Go 'Round
NY to LA
Oceans Away!
Out of the World (outer space)
Party in the USA
Pedal to the Metal
(The) Road
Rockin' Around the World
R-O-C-K in the USA
This Land Is Your Land
Traditions around the World
Turn the Radio Up!
(The) Wild West
World Dance Tour

GENERAL THEMES

All That Glitters
America's True Talent ...
And the Winner Is ...
(The) Art of Making Art
(The) Big Noise
Billboard Top 40
Eat, Drink, and Be MUSICAL!
Evening of Entertainment
Fire and Ice (hot and cold)
Friendship
Games People Play
Girls Just Wanna Have Fun
Good vs. Evil

Gotta Sing! Gotta Dance!
It's All Good
Let Me Entertain You
Lights, Camera, DANCE!
Lights, Camera, MUSIC!
Magic!
Magic and Music
Music and Passion
(The) Music in Me
Musical Potpourri
NPR—New Production Review
Off the Wall
Old Time Rock and Roll!
On Stage
One Night Only
Opening Night
Opposites Attract
Pure Imagination
Puttin' on the Glitz
Putting It Together
Rain or Shine (weather songs)
Razzle Dazzle
(The) Reviews Are In ...
Right as Rain
Rock and Roll Will Never Die
So You Think You Can Sing AND Dance!?!
Standing Room Only! (SRO)
Stop. Listen. GROW!
Take It Easy
This 'n' That!
Turn the Radio Up!
We Got the Beat!
What a Feeling!
Why We Sing
    (Greg Gilpin's "Why We Sing" as theme song)
Without a Song
Workin' Nine to Five
Working for a Living (occupations)

COMPOSER THEMES

All the Single Ladies (female composers)
Bach and Beyond ...
(A) *Barry* Good Show (*Barry Manilow*)
Berlin or Bust (*Bach, Bernstein, Beethoven, Brahms,
    The Beatles, Billy Joel*)
By George! It's *Gershwin*!

Elton and Elvis Forever

It's Delightful, It's De-lovely, It's ... *Porter* Time!

Just Jason (*Robert Brown*)

Ladies' Choice (female composers)

Lessons from *Lerner and Lowe*

Musical Memories from *Rodgers and Hammerstein* (or *Lerner and Lowe*)

(A) Night of *Gershwin* (or insert any composer)

(The) Sound of *Sinatra* (or *Sondheim*)

This Is It! (*Michael Jackson*)

SCHOOL COLORS AND MASCOT THEMES

Pick one of these themes and insert your school name, mascot or color.

Bear-lesque (for bears or grizzlies)

(The) Best of *Butler* (insert your school's name)

Bravo *Butler*

Bulldog Bash

Butler on Broadway

Crusaders in Concert

Eagle-antics

Gold Dust

(The) *Gorilla* Groove

Heritage High Harmonies

Husker (or *Hurricane* or *Hawkeyes*) Harmonies

Jazzin' with the *Jaguars*

Knights on Broadway

(A) Little *Knight* Music

Magic *Knights*

Maverick Melodies

Minute Men Melodies

Purple Reign (Prince)

Raven Review

Red-Hot *Razorbacks*!

Redskin Rhythms

Saint-sations

Silver Serenade

Singing *Saints*

Tiger Tunes

Wildcat Encore

CALENDAR THEMES

April Showers (Cloudburst; Trickle, Trickle)

Blessings!

(A) Boo-tiful Night

Celebrate America!

Circle of Friends

Count Your Blessings

(An) Evening of Love Songs

Everything's Comin' Up Music

Fall Is in the Air

Forever Autumn

(The) Four Seasons

Give My Regards to Springtime

Give Thanks

In Like a Lamb, Out Like Lionel Hampton

June Is Bustin' Out All Over

June Tunes

Love Is in the Air

March Musical Madness

(A) Musical Bouquet

Musical May Baskets (artwork using music notes spilling out of baskets)

New Generation

(A) Night of Hallowed Music

(A) Night of Tricks and Treats

Party Like It's 2999!

Raindrops Keep Fallin' on My Head

Red, White, and BLUES!

Rock Around the Clock

Rockin' Around the Calendar

School Daze

Seasons of Love

September Songs

Singing in the Rain

Those Were the Days

Tunes in June

Won't You Be My ♥ (Valentine)?

(A) Yankee Doodle Time

CHRISTMAS/WINTER THEMES

Baby, It's Cold Outside, But It's Warm in Here!

Candlelight Carols

Celebrate

Christmas Around the World

Christmas Journeys

(The) Gift

Have a "Barry" Merry Christmas

Hip-Hop Noel

Holiday Happenings

Holiday Inn

Holiday Magic!

Holidazzle

Holly Jolly Holidays

Home for the Holidays

I'm Dreaming of a ... Tropical Vacation!

Jazzy Jingles

Jingle Bell Hop

Joy to the World

Keepin' the "C" in Christmas

Let It Snow! Let It Snow! Let It Snow!

(The) Lighting of the Candles

Miracle on _____ Street (fill in school's street name here)

Nutcracker Sweets

Peppermint Follies

Reindeer Games

Santa's Frosty Follies

Season for Giving

Sleigh Bell Chills and Thrills

Snow Business like Show Business

'Til the Big Guy Sings

Twelve Days AFTER Christmas

Winter Wonderland

Wonders of the Season

MUSIC THEME IDEAS TO MIX AND MATCH

American Heroes

American Spectacular

Americana

Birth of ...

Bravo

Bring It On!

Carnival!

Celebrate America!

Celebrating ...

(The) Classics

Collage ...

Come Fly with Me or Come Dance with Me

Days of ...

Dream Big

Everyone Rejoice!

Festival of Music

Fiesta!

Generation Hooked on ...

Golden Age of ...

Good vs. Evil

Heroes

I'd Like to Teach the World to Sing

I'm a Little Bit Country/Rock and Roll

In Concert ...

In Praise of Music

Let Us Entertain You

Love ...

Love Train

Magic ...

Music! Music! Music!

Nickelodeon

Party ...

Portrait of ...

Proudly We Present

Rainbow ...

Refrains ...

Remembering ...

Reviewing ...

Rhythm of Life

Rhythm Rhapsody

... Rhythms

Sea to Shining Sea

Show Choir Spectacular

Show Time!

Showcase ...

Solid Gold!

Songs of the Spirit!

Tapestry

Tearin' Up the '30s and '40s

That's Entertainment

This Is My Country

To Everything There Is a Season

Tonight's the Night!

Touring ...

Turn the Beat Around

Twentiana

We Are the Music Makers

We Salute You

(Your Theme) Around the World

(Your Theme) on Parade

I'M JUST SAYING...

Use a song title from your opening number and build the theme around that title or musical opening line. "It's a Grand Night for Singing," "On Broadway," and "One!" are classics and could be used every year as a show opener. Bookend the show by using the opening song as the ending as well—finish with the last chorus and tag to pull the show together.

CHAPTER 4:
FROM THE PIT TO
THE OVERHEADS

THE COMBO

Even though I've worked with a collegiate instrumental combo for more than 25 years, I have learned the most playing keyboard and singing at the mic with our church praise team. Our instrumentalists and vocalists practice midweek and then again at 7 a.m. prior to the first Sunday morning service. Even though I'm a trained musician and know the importance of rehearsal, it wasn't until I bombed (putting it lightly) at the keyboard (during a baptism) that I had a revelation about actually being a vital part of an instrumental combo. I'm sure the congregation and the baby's family wished I'd had my revelation sometime before the service. Nonetheless, I am better for it and will share my findings.

Personally, I believe I am called to bring my best gifts to the altar, whether at church or school, or while writing a book! Many times we focus on the people up front (i.e., those at the mic or our singer/dancers) and forget about those who are truly the backbone of the music. The phrase "leave your ego at the door" should be tattooed on all our hands and hearts. Instrumentalists with servant spirits will fare better than those who are all about their own talents. Each member must understand his or her role in the performance. If more than one person tries to take the reins, the performance is headed for disaster. Listen to the person in charge. Just because you can play a walking bass line, arpeggiate to the nth degree, or think the piece needs more cowbell, don't do it. The combo must be one—one sound, one mind, one heart, and one tempo!

There is no substitute for live accompaniment. But, it does take extra time and training to put together the desired combo sound. Don't give only your leftover time or energies to the instrumentalists. Treat each member with respect and include them at all times. Cultivate unity on the team. If it works to put the instrumentalists in the spotlight for a brief moment, do so, but remind the combo that it is *not* their mission to be in front. The combo will be successful when everyone works as a team—wherever the placement on stage. If the director doesn't address the philosophy from the start, the program will not get off the ground.

Attitudes that hinder unity include narrow-mindedness and the belief that there is only one way to perform a number. Be cautious that egos don't get in the way. Inflated egos cause students to expect solos, disregard style and balance, and then become inflexible in rehearsal and performance. There is one director, and he or she gets to make all the decisions. Period. It is not a democracy. Even though the students may be asked to get involved in smaller decision-making, these decisions will not affect the importance or impact of the music program in a negative manner. The ideas may seem immense to the students and give more ownership to the participants in the program, but the students need to understand that they will always report back to the director for final decision-making.

Is there a perfect band member? A musician with the right talent, a passion for music, and a compassionate spirit is a great starting place. A student needs humble confidence, commitment

to rehearsals and performances, musical proficiency, and a pledge to take on daily individual practice. The qualifications of a band member match the qualifications for the perfect vocal ensemble member (and instructor). The achievements of an organization are the results of the combined effort of each individual.

> **The achievements of an organization are the results of the combined effort of each individual.**

RESPONSIBILITIES AND CHALLENGES OF INSTRUMENTALISTS—AND THEIR DIRECTORS—IN VOCAL ENSEMBLES

1) **Obtain music** from the director as soon as possible (the earlier the better).

2) Cut and paste the music to make page turns easier. Nonglare plastic sheet protectors in black spiral notebooks are a professional and easy way to store music.

3) Put music in show order in own folder.

4) Decide on transpositions (if using a different instrument) and mark accordingly.

5) Put music and instruments away after each rehearsal and leave the rehearsal area clean.

6) **Work individually and as a team** to learn notes, rhythms, and chords.

7) Rehearse individually, as a combo, and then with the singers.

8) Make stylistic changes to stay true to the original.

9) Take private lessons if you are lacking in an area—be a strong link in the chain.

10) **Add color and enhance groove** collectively.

11) Synthesizers add color and can create a sound closer to the original artist's audio.

12) Accessory percussion instruments can enhance the groove of a song (for example, congas, wood block, triangle, wind chimes, slide whistle, egg shakers, castanets, claves, cowbell, pie tins, spoons). Be creative; there are endless possibilities.

13) Pianists should use the left hand sparingly if a bass guitarist is present.

14) **Pay attention to texture and dynamics**.

15) When vocals are present, instrumentals must be soft. During unison vocal sections, instrumentalists should play out. When vocalists are singing four-part harmony, instrumentalists need to back off so the harmonies can be heard.

16) Instrumentalists should play out during dance breaks, interludes, and transitions. That is the time when the combo can shine and really ROCK OUT!!

17) More separation (staccato) and less legato may help to enhance the vocals.

18) Instrumentalists should use a variety of ranges, not duplicating or playing in unison with the vocal line except for occasional color considerations.

19) Remember, all combo members should not be playing all of the time. Mix it up.

20) **Be aware of the rhythmic and harmonic structures** as they change.

21) Use less rhythmic and chordal "busyness" with complex vocals.

22) Save the complex fills for when vocalists are sustaining notes. *Oohs* and *ahhs* or simpler vocal lines encourage intricate combo accompaniment.

23) Each piece needs to have rhythmic and harmonic variety throughout. If the piece is demanding from start to end, it will exhaust the audience.

24) **Accent dance moves** and special choreography.

25) Cymbals, bass drum, rim shots and hits work well as accents. Although percussion is the primary method for accents, other instruments also can be used to bring attention to certain moves.

26) Ask the combo to watch the choreography, penciling in special dance moves in the score. This will help the focus during shows, will give ownership as they work as a team to enhance the accompaniment, and will add percussive energy to the dance.

27) Rhythmically punch out certain syncopations. Use very little sustaining pedal and cut down on pads (sustained synthesizer or guitar sounds), which easily could cover vocals.

28) **Rehearse the introduction and the ending** before rehearsing the number in entirety.

29) Getting started and stopped can be tricky for every member of the ensemble. Rehearse tempo changes and work to quickly get in the groove of each number.

30) Write in all tags, repeats, and dynamics.

31) Understand when and if transition or bowing music is used.

32) **Work the tempos and be flexible** in performance; stay aware of tempo-influencing factors.

33) Vocals, choreography, and audience reaction can dictate tempo.

34) Audience age, size of the crowd, time of day, and performing space are factors that can dictate tempo. The response or energy level of performers and/or audience can also dictate the tempo. Don't go on automatic pilot.

35) Watch the conductor. Don't try to second-guess the director. Trust and respect the director's decisions at all times.

36) **Listen and blend.**

37) Monitors and other sound issues can affect the blend.

38) Sound checks are essential. Be sure to communicate with the director and the sound technician respectfully.

39) Lighter colors in instrumentation (for example, flute rather than brass) help the balance. Save brass for big dance breaks or for punches.

40) **Consider pacing** of the program.

41) The combo can make or break the sequencing. Members must think ahead.

42) If the show order is changed from venue to venue, the tempos of each piece will also vary. It is about the flow of the show. Live audiences add challenges. Transitions can be used for costume changes, set changes, introductions, scene changes, and setting the mood.

43) **Think about combo placement** for your ensemble.

44) If several ensembles are performing in one single performance, decide the best place to set up the combo. Changing or moving instruments in the middle of a production wreak havoc with programming and the pacing of a show. If you reset the stage, there is a chance that cords and sound equipment won't get plugged back in correctly.

45) The bass player and amplifier should be placed in the center of the rhythm section for all to hear, as the bass is the core of the unit and provides the pulse.

46) If the combo is not set up to see the singers, place a TV monitor in front of the combo. This can take care of a multitude of possible problems.

47) **Make a lesson plan for the combo**. The instrumentalists can't improve unless they know what to fix musically. If "hitting correct notes" is all you and the players are concerned with, rehearsals will be boring rather than musically challenging for the instrumentalists.

48) Coordinate the combo's and the singers' lesson plans. Then, when all the musicians join together, listen for the improved sound.

49) Leave individual notes for the students. It may take a few minutes but will be well worth the trouble. Add a "Rockstar" energy drink or "Extra" gum for the superstar band.

50) **Always remember that we are in the business of music education**—not show business. Don't hurt a budding musician or sacrifice a fragile ego if possible. Always teach in love.

I'M JUST SAYING...

Treat your combo members with the utmost respect. Appreciate what each individual combo member brings to the plate. Give credit to your band members whenever possible. To validate their importance to the singers, ask combo members to drop out in the middle of a selection. Notice that the singers may tune better when the bass is playing or have added energy with a drum set. The band is the glue that holds the groove together. Give the members their time to shine by building in a special moment at the end of your show to allow them the accolades due.

BASIC TECHNIQUES AND SKILLS TO ENHANCE THE COMBO SOUND AND ENSEMBLE:

Piano/Keyboard

• Listen to the style of the piece.

• The piano should be used to fill, not to double parts.

• Playing too busily may detract from—or even cover—the choral sound.

• Playing in different octaves will add additional color(s).

• Use a metronome in rehearsal. It will frustrate the singers and the band at first, but this exercise may prove that the singers rush the tempo. Rarely do singers slow down tempo.

• Be cautious of overusing the sustaining pedal. If the playing is too legato, it is difficult to hear the rhythmic energy and the singers' enunciation, and lyrics will be muddy.

- If the bass (string or guitar) has a walking bass line, the pianist should use very little left hand. Let the bass take over. The arrangement will not be tight if the bass doubles the piano.

- Watch out for "octavitis." (Don't repeat what any other instrument is playing!)

- Rehearse exactly as you'll be performing. Don't make changes right before or during a show.

- Remember that accompanying an ensemble is different from performing as a piano soloist.

- Always mark your part. You will not remember changes in the heat of battle. But use a pencil, not a pen. Directors and choreographers are known to change their minds.

- Prepare your score with as few page turns as possible. Use clothespins or heavy cardstock if the performance takes place outside. Be ready for whatever Mother Nature throws your way.

Bass Guitar
- One of the main functions of the bass guitar is to "set the groove."

- Ensemble pitch improves as singers tune to the bass guitar.

- Bass guitar should be felt as much as heard.

- Keep the volume down on the amp. The bass sound carries.

- The kick drums and bass guitar should practice alone together. If they are solid, your singers will also be rock-solid. The ensemble will never be solid if the piano, bass, and drums aren't together.

- Always have a tuner in arm's distance for the guitarist.

- Low bass sounds can swallow vocals. Equalize the bass low and treble high.

- In planning a chord change, think of the easiest way to get there.

- If you have a good bass player, trust him or her. Adding instruments will muddy up the bass line.

- Offer rhythmic challenges. Pull out the bass line if balance is off.

- Work on achieving a clear but mellow sweet sound for jazz. Use the gravelly sound for rock.

- If a bass guitar instrument or player is not available, a synthesizer can be substituted. The sound is close to the actual sound and a person with keyboard experience can accompany.

- The amp is half the instrument and could be problematic. Teach the bass player to control the amp.

Electric Guitar
- The electric guitar serves two functions: rhythmic and melodic fills.

- Ask the guitarist to pull back a bit, as the electric guitar goes out of tune quickly.

- Suggest that the guitarist try a rhythmically muted part.

- Guitar and bass can play octave lines together on high-energy songs.

- Use distorted power chords to boost chorus energy.

- Don't add extra notes and noise to a delicate ballad.

- Allow the guitarist and drummer to set up certain styles selected by the director.

- The electric guitar should give harmonic support and improvisational fills. Except on rare occasions, it shouldn't duplicate the piano and bass lines.

Drums/Percussion

- Most drummers would rather use the "real deal"—that is, a drum set instead of an electronic set. Arguments can be made for both sides. Use an electronic set if you absolutely cannot hear the singers over the drum; otherwise, use an acoustic set and keep your drummer happy.

- Consider the drummer as the motor of the band. The drummer's jobs are to keep time and to support and set up rhythmic structures of the songs.

- Cymbals can drown out choral sound. In the 1970s, drummers used masking tape on the underside edge of the cymbal and peeled back the tape an inch at a time, limiting the sustain. If the singers continue to be covered up by the cymbal sound, threaten the drummer with this little bit of trivia and a roll of masking tape. Less "after ring" is a better choice of cymbal for vocalists.

- Fills are normally played at the end or top of a section. Be careful of timing. Do not play a fill over a vocal or an instrumental solo.

- A cross-stick on the snare drum is used during laid-back sections of songs or particular styles like country, folk, reggae, rock, and jazz.

- Hits are used to emphasize parts of a song. They are usually played in conjunction with the entire band. Ask the drummer to watch the choreography and accent any sudden, large punches in the choreography. This technique should be used sparingly.

- Drummers may or may not be required to start a number with a count-in depending on the director. Drummers set tempo and style and can bring in the singers with stick clicks on counts 5-6-7-8 or a rhythmic cadence.

- Offer rhythmic challenges in all the instrumental parts, not just with percussion.

- Endings—the last note of a song is what people tend to remember most. Watch the director closely for signal of chorus ending. Drummers act as a signal to the rest of the band. The song needs to conclude with a fitting percussion ending. Make it tight and defined. Definite shots, ritardandos, punctuation marks, cymbal swells, and trashcan endings (potatoes rolling down the stairs) are a few forms that drummers use to signal the big finish.

- A ballad's closing measures might use a bell tree or brushes on a cymbal.

- Watch out for "cymbalitis," or too much cymbal. Make your crashes count!

Balancing the Drums

- To make drums sound good, sometimes the drummer must play louder. That normally doesn't work because of the balance issues. Try a plexiglass (acrylic glass) shield or an electronic drum set if all else fails.

- If your drummers play too loud (which often happens with school-age drummers), ask them to use brushes, or a soft felt beater on the bass drum pedal. Instead of snare sticks or brushes, drummers can use multi-rods or bamboo dowels.

- If a drummer is still playing too loud, fill the bass drum with shredded polyfoam or pillows.

- The plexiglass shield will redirect sound but not necessarily soak up or soften the percussive sound.

- Ear monitors for drummers might be worth the price. Ask a sound expert for more information.

- When purchasing a drum kit, it might be wise to buy a jazz kit. It will have a smaller kick drum and smaller toms.

To make a plexiglass drum shield: Buy three or four sheets (depending on desired size) of two-foot-by-five-foot segments of plexiglass. (If you want the shield to curve, you will need at least three sheets of plexiglass.) Drill starter holes (pilot holes) or the acrylic sheets might crack. Use door hinges so the shield can be moved in and out of classroom and onto a stage by simply removing the hinge pins. Talk to someone who uses a comparable drum shield before investing in one of your own.

Synthesizer

- Listen to recordings to see how to orchestrate for the synthesizer.

- Let the combo rehearse separately in a different space or time.

- Concentrate on the director's preparatory beat for attacks and releases.

- Electric piano sound is especially nice for soft ballads.

- Strings can be used to fill in and make the sound more majestic on almost any song, or for soft ballads.

- Use sustaining pedal, as it will make the lines smoother.

- Play open, long, held lines; arpeggiate when the line dictates more movement and exhilarating instrumentation.

- Pad is primarily a sustaining sound in an otherwise rhythmic world.

- Create the rock-style organ stop by using two fingers in right hand and use the modulation wheel to create the natural vibrato of an organ. Grace notes and glissandos work well on these kinds of parts.

- Contrast is desired for every musical selection. Think of colors and sounds adding more variety in the show.

- Trumpet and brass work well for shots and fanfares. Brass can also be used for exciting dance breaks.

- Do not overorchestrate. Be sensitive to adding color while not ruining balance with the singers.

Acoustic Guitar

- Listen to lots of CDs to figure out the style that you want to emulate. Develop your own style.

- A capo (padded bar placed across the fingerboard of the guitar) can add to the effect of the piece by creating different tonal textures. It also helps the singer (and guitarist) figure out the best key.

- If you put the capo up, you'll get a sound like a mandolin.

- Learn to finger pick if you're playing acoustic guitar.

- Buy a guitar tuner. You will not regret the expense.

Instrumentalists should follow the same rules as the singers. Remove hats when rehearsing so the director can see your eyes. Protect instruments and professionalism by honoring thy neighbor, other combo members, and the director!

It is imperative that the combo rehearses alone before accompanying the singers. This will give the singers time for sectionals and independence on the vocal parts and allow both groups a positive experience the first time the groups get together to rehearse. If combo members are onstage during a show, they need to smile and use professional decorum as the audience will focus on them—even when they are in silhouette. The combo should not outshine the singers but rather complement them. Be sure that singers thank the combo at the end of each rehearsal.

I'M JUST SAYING...

During one particularly rough rehearsal, the instrumentalists and singers were having difficulty matching energies. I came to the conclusion that when a singer gets tired, he or she sings softer and dances slower, but when the instrumentalist get tired, he or she plays faster and louder. It was one of those "A-HA!" moments. The human voice is fragile and has to be treated with respect. It cannot compete with all the electric sounds, amps, reverberating drum sets, and monitors with lots of woofers.

A BALANCING ACT

Understandable lyrics are among the biggest challenges for directors, choreographers, combo directors, sound crew, and the audience. If your audience can't understand the lyrics, your message is lost. The director should walk around the performing space to make sure that the singers are projecting words and can be heard over the combo.

Balance is important and must be resolved. Remind the singers that if the section is *forte*, they need to dance *forte*. If the section is *piano*, they need to dance with a softer energy level. Instrumentalists can play out during dance breaks, punches, and transitions. The bow should be the loudest part of the show for the combo, but should not hit rock and roll decibels. Always perform with regard to the age and maturity of the audience. If children are plugging their ears and/or seniors are wincing and turning down their hearing aids, the audience is not having a positive performance experience.

Finding **balance in life** has always been challenging for me. I know this section was originally to be about balancing the performer's sound, but I want to take it a step further and share a "life lesson" I teach my students each year. Butler alums come back year after year to say thanks for this advice and I know it is effective. I call it "balancing your pyramid." This idea came from a friend, David Connolly, in November 1997. I have used the philosophy every day since then. In a nutshell, a personal pyramid has four sides: mental, physical, emotional, and spiritual. To remain healthy and productive, a person needs to grow those four areas daily. When one of the sides gets out of whack or is completely ignored, the pyramid collapses.

Mental: Learn something new every day. Good students never stop growing. Good teachers never stop growing! Try something new and don't be afraid to fail. You will learn much in the process. Set aside time for daily quiet time and reading—even if only for five minutes.

Physical: Fit exercise and a healthy diet into your lifestyle. Take care of your body daily. What you put into the body is what you become. If you want your body to last, don't start bad habits. Smoking, alcohol abuse, illegal substances, and inadequate nutrition will hinder your growth as a musician and as a person.

Emotional: Emotions are automatic and can't be controlled. We can, however, control our responses. Love and fear are the two basic underlying emotions, and all other emotions stem from these two sentiments. To be successful in life, we must learn to deal with our emotions.

Spiritual: This is the most personal of all. The soul has to be fed daily. Students will have to figure this out individually through quiet time and reading. Find time to grow spiritually. Lack of a spiritual life can lead to disease and illness.

I'M JUST SAYING...

We all want our students to be successful and happy. We also know that most of them will not make their living as singers, dancers, or anything connected to this crazy art of music. However, I hope that students will obtain life lessons over time as they participate in my ensembles. If they stay in the habit of keeping their personal pyramids balanced, they will have a better chance of living life to the fullest and enjoying the future, whatever their career choices.

SOUND CHECKS

Sound checks can be a really frustrating topic—frustrating because no matter how much the ensemble rehearses, prepares, and tries to prevent pilot error, it seems as if something always goes wrong during the performance. It reminds me of the year I coached the drill team as well as served as the high school's vocal instructor/choreographer/accompanist/counselor/fundraiser. Without fail, ballgame after ballgame, the same sound bloopers would occur during the halftime entertainment. The dancers would walk out to the middle of the field and/or court and patiently wait for the music to start. There they would stand awkwardly, waiting and waiting to hear the intro, for what seemed like an eternity. Finally, the music—several measures past the song's beginning—would blare through the loudspeaker. The girls would panic in confusion. Some would run around trying to find their spot in the choreography and the formation. A few would try to signal the announcer to start the music over, and others would just run off in tears.

I would give the dancers my solemn vow that it would all be fixed for the next performance. Lo and behold, the next time I would get up to the press box, some person would have inadvertently switched cords, turned off power, spilled soda on the cables, or, for the seventeenth game in a row, forgotten that the dancers were standing out there waiting for the music cue. I know you have all seen a scenario like the one I just described. Unfortunately, even with careful rehearsal and sound preparation, it still happens.

> ### Performers must be taught proper microphone technique.

So, do we just accept fate and forget about trying to rehearse before the show with microphones and sound checks? Most definitely not! Students need to feel comfortable onstage. They need to be taught proper microphone technique. Remind the students to be thankful for the sound crew (or the volunteering parent or staff member) that is helping to better their show. Also, teach professional behavior. Explain that technical equipment sometimes has a mind of its own. Many times, the squeals, screeches, or silence are not the engineer's fault; rather, the blame lies with antiquated or inadequate equipment, lack of rehearsal time, or other sound issues.

In the show choir arena, hanging mics overhead or putting mics up front will often give the show choir a general boost. Soloists normally use hand-held mics or step up to a front microphone. If done properly, this setup helps increase the sound and projection of the singers.

Amplification is used to project the sound and also to create a presence in the room. Our ears aren't used to hearing acoustic sounds, but rather, amplified sounds. As we walk through the grocery store, wait in the doctor's office, sit in restaurants, or watch movies and TV, we hear sound that has been changed. Therefore, our sound must go through the amps and speakers to create a more professional-sounding choir—the sound that we are accustomed to hearing.

I'M JUST SAYING...

My advice would be to find a person or company you feel comfortable with for professional sound advice. Every sound situation is unique. It is a shame when students work and rehearse for weeks on end, only to not be heard because of unfortunate sound problems that could have been avoided with proper planning and preparations.

MIC TECHNIQUE

Here are some ideas to improve the overall sound of your group. These are basic ideas; there are many sound and mic variables for each performance venue.

MIC TECHNIQUE FOR "SOUNDING" GOOD IN THE SHOW

- A trained operator or someone with experience should be used at all times.
- The sound engineer needs to throw away the headphones for much of the performance as he or she should hear what the audience hears. Headphones should be used in troubleshooting. If a "hot" voice suddenly pops through, or if a blaring intonation problem surfaces and it is a mystery where the sounds are coming from, that is the time to pull out headphones.
- Remind the singers that what they sing into the mic is what the audience hears. If the performers sing out of tune or don't enunciate, that is exactly what comes over the sound system. As Stephen Todd, a rising star in show choir choreography, says so eloquently, "Poop in, poop out." That may be a bit crass, but I guarantee you won't forget that bit of advice.
- Tune your sound system. Bring in a professional who can work with EQ (equalization). EQ is the process of using passive or active electronic elements for the purpose of "flattening" the frequencies.
- Ask the sound engineer to anticipate the soloists at the microphones. Give written information on the soloists to the sound engineer. After a good sound check, the audience should never miss hearing a soloist.
- The sound engineer needs to keep one eye on the stage, one eye on the program, and ears open at all times.
- Encouragement should be given to the engineers running sound as well as to the soloists who are performing. Give them a preferred example for sound. It is tough for them to make choices when they don't have a concept of the sound the director is wanting.
- If the soloist can't hear, ask the sound engineer to put a hot spot monitor in front of him or her. The hot spot monitors are small, generally inexpensive, and easy to move on the stage.
- Use monitors for the vocalists.
- Vocalists should hear vocal, piano, and bass in the monitors; that is enough.
- Sound check exactly as you would for the performance. Don't leave anything to chance (please use risers with choreography, sing with full voices, have faces on, have all instruments playing, etc.). Any little change can potentially have an effect on the sound.
- Rehearse with the mic stands. The one-hand squeeze-triggered mic stand is easy to adjust quickly. It allows you to grip with one hand and do a fast height adjustment on the fly while being durable and long lasting.
- Stay close and think about "kissing the mic." With most mics, practice turning your head and keeping the mic close to your lips. If you move your head without the mic, you might lose sound. Don't wait until show time to practice mic technique. Use painted dowel rods or thick magic markers in lieu of actual microphones for rehearsals.
- Keep the sound engineer in the house. The engineer needs to hear what the audience hears.
- Practice mic passes. Make it a part of the choreography. Practice with mics from day one. Don't add anything the day of the show, no matter how easy it seems.
- Draw on the soundboard to get greater dynamic contrast in your show.

I'M JUST SAYING...

I'm guessing this has happened to every teacher out there, but just in case it hasn't, take time to laugh and then take note. If you, the teacher/director, are sporting a headpiece mic that's all taped in but you need to use the restroom or speak confidentially with a performer backstage, either remember to turn off your mic or make sure the sound person stays alert at all times and turns off the microphone. Let's just say, there was one intermission NO ONE in the house will forget. ☺ Luckily, we all have these hilarious stories to share. Right!?!?

FEEDBACK

Feedback is defined as a piercing hum (often described as squealing, screeching, or ringing) sometimes heard with sound systems. Feedback can be caused when certain frequencies come out of the speaker and go back through the microphone again, making a looped signal. In layman's terms, feedback occurs when the signal travels in a continuous loop. One of the most common feedback situations is shown in the diagram below. A microphone sends a signal into the mixer (or sound system), which then amplifies and sends out the signal from the speaker, which is picked up again by the microphone.

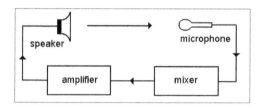

To eliminate feedback, you must interrupt the feedback loop.

SUGGESTIONS FOR CONTROLLING FEEDBACK

- Use a directional microphone.
- Change the position of the microphone and/or speaker so that the speaker isn't feeding directly into the mic.
- Keep speakers in front of the microphones, i.e., speakers closer to the audience.
- Speaker monitors can also contribute to making the sound muddy.
- Kiss the microphone when singing. Keep mouth an inch or so in proximity at all times. (This rule won't apply for every type of mic. Ask the sound technician for advice.)
- Check to see that the volume (gain) isn't at the highest level. If the singer stays close to the mic, the gain can be reduced and, therefore, you'll have less chance of feedback.
- Turn off the microphone when not in use. But be sure the next soloist remembers to turn it back on. Believe it or not, forgetting to turn on the mic is one of the biggest sound blunders and causes sound techs more grief than almost anything else.
- Lower the speaker output, so the microphone doesn't pick it up.
- Avoid aiming speakers directly at walls, as they act as reflective surfaces. The sound will bounce around in smaller areas and off hard walls.

- Use direct feeds instead of microphones for bass guitar, guitar, and synthesizer.
- Train soloists to turn away from or walk away from speakers if they hear feedback.
- If you can afford in-ear monitors and your instrumentalists will be open to change, try them instead of speaker monitors.

Some guitarists actually make use of controlled feedback for artistic reasons. This is what's happening when a guitarist holds his/her guitar up close to a speaker. Voilà!

Of course, many situations result in feedback. The use of monitors means additional potential feedback problems. That is why your performers need tech rehearsals before each and every performance—with everyone there! **Buy good sound equipment and either train a student or hire a professional to run the equipment.**

A DIFFERENT KIND OF FEEDBACK

This isn't the typical sound problem that you normally find in a feedback and sound section. This feedback story took place with my church choir last spring. After rehearsing a selection for the annual Easter cantata, the tenors were struggling with the high range of the piece. Week after week the tenors complained that they couldn't sing that high—it didn't "sound" natural. My accompanist and I listened to them moan and wail for several weeks. (Deep down, I think we enjoyed knowing that they were being tormented just a little. After all, these ornery tenors were the ones who played practical jokes on us in rehearsals, making up "back-row doo-wop choreography" and threatening to add cowbell to some of our favorite anthems.)

Finally, we decided to compromise. Instead of switching to a simpler piece, we would indulge the tenors by transposing the piece down a minor third. This decision made the tenors ecstatic, while the altos and basses were a bit skeptical. However, once we tried the anthem in the new key, everyone was satisfied. We could sing the anthem and it would indeed work for the Easter service, just a few days away.

Easter morning came and the choir faithfully gathered before the worship service. Normally we would do a run-through right before the service, to warm up voices and remember any little changes made in rehearsal. Since everything had gone so smoothly at the last practice, I felt as if the choir was in great shape. Heck, they didn't even need to warm up, as the piece was in a lower range for everyone. For once, I suggested that we save the singers' voices and minds for the actual worship service, keeping the cantata anthem fresh. I reminded them to let their faces express what they were feeling so that the congregation could enjoy the message through song.

The worship service soon began. It came time in the service to present our anthem, and, instead of taking time to get situated, I hurriedly motioned to our accompanist to begin the introduction. She quickly pushed buttons on the Clavinova, transposing the piece. Once she began playing, I knew we were in trouble. I had to quickly decide whether to start over or act as if nothing was wrong, preserving the flow of the service. I prayed the choir would be so focused on the lyrics that they wouldn't notice the "change." I smiled and brought in the choir on their cue.

Once the vocals started, it was evident to all the singers that something was drastically different. In the hurry to get started, I hadn't given our accompanist time to look at the transposition buttons. Instead of transposing the piece a minor third down, the piece was transposed a minor third up instead. The entire choir was singing three full steps higher than we had rehearsed. The entire cantata sat right in the tenors' falsetto range.

If only I had a video of the ensemble. First, eyes widened, then shoulders started creeping up, and finally faces turned red from the breath and energy being expended.

Are you curious about the feedback from the congregation after the service? They loved the energy in the faces and the huge smiles from each and every choir member. Don't view feedback and sound problems as always having a negative connotation. If you keep singing, maybe no one will notice!

And to this day, the entire church choir gets the giggles when the tenors complain about high notes. I always threaten … do you want us to transpose the piece for you!?

LIGHT THE LIGHTS

Theatrical lighting can add excitement and energy to any show choir performance, as long as it fulfills the primary function of **letting the audience see the show**. How much is concealed or revealed by the lighting is the director's decision. Let your concert lighting be a more creative part of the show and not become stale or appear basic. Think more in terms of devising lights for a musical and less "lights on … lights off."

Designing lights for the show choir requires **imagination**; turning ideas into reality requires careful lighting choices and a basic understanding and knowledge of light and color concepts. **Lighting placement** is crucial for good visual effects, as the main purpose of lighting is to illuminate the stage and the performers. It won't matter how brilliant your choreography is if no one can see it because the stage is too dark. The lighting technicians control the show (or world—whichever is the case).

Basic fixture types include **spotlights** for focused lighting of individual performers, **floodlights** for illuminating larger areas, and **special effect lighting**. (In most cases, if your school possesses special effect lighting, you would have your own lighting designer and wouldn't need to read this chapter in the first place.)

Floodlights and spotlights should include various gel color filters. The primary goal is to make certain the entire stage is covered in light. The most inexpensive and efficient light to do this is the floodlight. It is a shame to spend so much time on other show details and not be concerned about some of the final technical aspects of the performance.

Top light and side light can add "plasticity" to the performance when combined with front light in the right proportions and color combinations. Use **special lighting effects** in moderation. If the effects are overused, they won't be much of a surprise for the audience. The first time a group uses strobe lights in a number, it is very effective. Using strobe lights again soon after that performance negates the shock value. The audience will soon expect certain things. Keep 'em in suspense!

A fog machine is another theatrical device that can drastically change lighting. Fog machines cause the beams to stand out, greatly enhancing any lighting effects. In addition, the fog makes light appear solid and/or in columns. A fog chiller keeps the fog closer to the ground, creating more of a rolling fog. This type of fog has a cloudlike appearance and can give a rather ethereal appearance.

Lighting can **enhance the costumes**. Mixing a few blue lights in with the natural lights can help make a blue costume look more blue (or "pop" on stage); adding red lights creates a more vivid red costume; and so forth. This is the X = X theory as it pertains to color and light. Costume colors, fabrics, backdrops, props, and decorations can all be affected by the lighting. It is a good idea to have a dress/tech rehearsal a few nights before the opening of a show. Those new costumes or even skin tones might not be the shade expected once the performers are illuminated.

Don't forget about the preshow. Make audience members feel special and welcomed as they enter the theater. Stage lights can cast a **glow on the set** before the show begins. A spotlight with a gobo (stencil) containing the theme of the show or the school's logo could be flashed on the back curtain. This feeling of anticipation will keep the audience guessing and ready to get on with the show!

TURN UP THE SPOTLIGHT

Spotlights can help guide the audience to focus where they should be focused. The light of the follow spot should find the soloist a few seconds before he or she begins singing. The spotlight operator must rehearse the light cues. If not, a serious moment can turn into somewhat of a comedy bit if the spotlight can't find the soloist.

The size and intensity of the spotlight should change depending on the type of solo. The light may expand as the piece gets more electrifying. It may narrow to a pin spot, a small circle of light outlining the face as the ballad fades away. The size of the light should be rehearsed so the soloist finds the light and doesn't move out of it.

If the entire body is illuminated, the bottom edge of the light will just touch the floor. Be aware of getting the final gesture totally in the spotlight. If arms are outstretched to the skies, make sure the spot picks up the entire body. To be on the safe side, use two spotlights to cover a person in light. And remember, if the rest of the stage is already well lit and flooded with light, spots may or may not be useful. The background must be darker than the spotlight.

One of my favorite effects with spotlights is the figure eight circling spots used during a kick line or a type of fanfare opening. You can just hear the drumroll as you read these words, can't you? It is another lighting device to build suspense and excitement in the theater.

SOME OF MY FAVORITE THEATRICAL LIGHTING "TOYS"

- **Backlight**: Simply means "light that comes from behind." On a conventional theater stage, this means lights that are hung upstage and shine back toward the audience.

- **Black light**: Darkened stage and "black lighting" (UV light), paired with fluorescent costumes, white gloves, or fluorescent makeup, will create visual illusions. The bulbs of the black lights should <u>not</u> be visible to the audience, as the UV light can give people headaches over an extended period of time.

- **Blackout**: Lights go to black suddenly. Be sure to use glow tape or lights backstage for performer's safety.

- **Christmas tree lights:** These can be used behind a scrim and will look like stars in the sky. It's an elegant look on trees for decorations, or you can use a battery-packed set on a person (as in "My Strongest Suit" from *Aida*).

- **Disco ball:** Let the spotlight hit it and watch it work. Fun for any '70s-type or disco-flavored music.

- **Dry ice:** Great effect. Put hot water in a container and drop in the dry ice for instant low fog. Can be purchased at most grocery stores or supermarkets. Caution: It can instantly freeze skin, and too much could make the floor slippery.

- **Flashlights**: Cover flashlight lenses with tissue paper (red and green for Christmas colors; add yellow for a stoplight). Can be used on stage as props or, in a movie theme, as penlights for the "ushers."

- **Gels in spotlights**: Gel in a spotlight will make a performer look completely different.

- **Gobos**: A theatrical gobo refers to a metal stencil placed over a light to create an image on the wall or other surface. If your school has little or no budget for technical effects, a pie plate could be used and the pattern cut with a knife. Gobos can be used on the stage floor to add texture to the stage, enhancing the performer's movements.

- **Rope light**: Inexpensive and safe to use on the floor or risers. Because of fire codes, the rope lights cannot stay installed between shows. Available in flashing and chasing lights, rope lights are extremely versatile.

- **Strobe lights**: A device to produce regular light flashes. Be cautious when using strobe lighting, as the effect can cause migraine headaches or epileptic seizures. Signs should be posted outside the theater to warn audience members anytime strobe lighting is used.

SCENERY AND PROPS

When "prop"-erly used (couldn't resist!), scenery and props are highly effective. Sets and backdrops add color and style changes, and will greatly enhance the mood you are trying to achieve. Traveling show choirs need to figure out the logistics of hauling, loading, and unloading equipment and then determine if scenery is worth the extra effort. Even if you don't use them while traveling, consider scenery and the stage set for home shows. This is just one more aspect that adds dimension to your program.

More than likely, you and your students won't have the time, desire, or resources to create the professional look needed. Art and theater students, faculty, or the entire department might be willing to collaborate on a "fine arts" project. A music booster club or a talented parent might also be willing to lend a hand. After the project is completed, remember to thank the responsible individuals with a written thank-you in the program and with a thank-you gift if you hope to continue the partnership. Thank-you texts or e-mails are not as meaningful as handwritten notes. Be sure to include people who donated time, supplies, talents, and manpower. A thank-you can go a long way for future relationships.

Props are an excellent way to add interest to the show. When props are added to the mix, rehearse with them weeks before the first show, not just a few days prior to the performance. Props need to be repaired between shows and should be in good working condition. A good rule of thumb is that the choreography and the vocals must be in great shape before students "earn" their props. If adding props, think BIG! Props need to read to the back of the house and into the balcony. Do not let the audience see the props until the exact time they are revealed.

And yet, sometimes it is fun to see students pantomiming as if they actually had the items in hand. You must be a great actor to make the tipping of a hat and swinging of a cane look believable to the audience. It can be exciting to the audience to "see" the imaginary prop if the pantomime is performed in a convincing manner.

The simplest object often makes an effective prop. Chairs, stools, and scaffolds can be used in a variety of ways to produce levels. The sky (and your budget) is the limit. Car dealerships often get rid of huge American flags. These make great backdrops for a patriotic number. If all else fails, rent, borrow, buy, or steal (I didn't say that!) backdrops, sets, and props.

Special effects must enhance the show. Be sure the effect makes the message stronger and communicates what the director is trying to achieve. If it causes the pacing of the show to be slowed or interrupted, or if it means there is not enough time to rehearse, think twice before throwing special effects together. If the performer has to do a crisscross on stage, do it to the prop, not after getting the prop. Just like singing and dancing, working with props takes some time to do right. Decide what the budgeted time allows and then plan accordingly.

I'M JUST SAYING...

Without a doubt, my favorite prop I've used on stage was my daughter, Stevie, at age four weeks. I held her in my arms as the Butler Headliners serenaded her and put her to sleep with Billy Joel's "Lullaby" at our final spring concert. I think I still have the VHS recording. Me, a stage mom? Whatever gave you that idea!?!

CHAPTER 5:
PUTTIN' ON THE GLITZ

COSTUMES

An audience first *sees* what they imagine an ensemble's sound will be. Dress for success. If you dress professionally, you'll be treated that way. Costumes must be functional and comfortable. Some of these costume tips may seem like common sense, but students need to be reminded of basic guidelines.

> **If you dress professionally, you'll be treated that way.**

Decide if your costumes will be jeans and T-shirts, decade styles, tuxes and ball gowns, or edgy and modern attire. Maybe your show will involve costume changes and the students will wear a combination of these styles. Clothing should fit the style of the music and choreography. A "Fred and Ginger" number needs an elegant look, but a hip-hop number requires tennis shoes, a backward baseball hat, a hoodie, and unique and individual street clothing. A country-and-western number would require something altogether different.

If your program calls for costume changes, be sure you have a reason for the change. The change must seem magical. It must happen quickly and the audience shouldn't be aware of any changes taking place. Suddenly, students appear on stage in new costumes and vibrant color pops. Voilà—presto chango—magic! If students leave stage, they shouldn't re-enter wearing the exact same costume they wore before, or why exit the stage? If it is not possible to change costumes, students could bring back a prop (add a tux coat, remove the tux coat, or add a vest; put on glasses, white gloves, boas, headpieces, or hats; carry on umbrellas or stools; and so on) to add visual interest.

It would be easy to fall prey to allowing revealing clothing to be worn onstage. Students may argue that it is all the rage, is available, and must be OK because "every other show choir in the world is wearing it!" "…*and if they were jumping off a cliff?*"

Add a few inches to skirts when ordering or sewing the hems. The audience may be seated a few feet below the stage. Patrons will be looking up and hem lengths will appear two inches shorter than they really are. Insist on proper undergarments for all students.

Stand firm in the wholesome, all-American look onstage. Every member of the ensemble needs to feel comfortable and look good in the clothing that is chosen. Audience members should feel comfortable when looking at the performers on stage. If the director is not comfortable commenting on stage clothing, invite a parent, a colleague, or a principal to get involved in the decision making.

Bright colors can wash out faces on stage. Choose a costume that looks good on all sizes. Material that moves, sways, or isn't stiff or unnatural works best. Use one and only one seamstress. Costumes will not have a uniform look if different people are interpreting "the" pattern. Directors and parents will spend countless hours and additional money trying to get a standardized look on stage.

I'M JUST SAYING…

My first year of teaching, I selected a short white dress as a costume for the show choir ladies. Coming from a dance and pageant background, I also insisted on nude color spankies (trunks) to be worn under the white dresses. After our first home show, several moms called our dean to complain that the ladies were not wearing any undergarments. I thought I was being clever and at the forefront of the fashion trend using the skin-tone color. I quickly reordered white spankies and the problem was resolved.

EXTENDING THE COSTUME CLOSET

Costume add-ons can be inexpensive and effective. If a chorus wants to start simply and add on, here is a great look and a fun way to be creative on stage. Males can start with black pants and white shirts; ladies can wear black leotards or black shirts and skirts. This basic dance costume can be embellished depending on the style of the number and choreography. A soloist or the entire ensemble can benefit from costume add-ons.

POSSIBLE COSTUME ADD-ONS
- **Aprons:** cooking style, fine waiters, *Hello Dolly*-style, art aprons, Dorothy apron, pilgrim, chef, clerk.
- **Bandannas:** cowboy style around the neck, street-dancing style on the forehead, around the arm, around the leg, in pocket as a hankie.
- **Famous celebrity masks or costumes:** Village People, Sonny and Cher, Beatles, John Travolta, Lady Gaga, Elvis Presley, Cleopatra, Marilyn Monroe, Dolly Parton, Madonna, Elton John, Michael Jackson, Betty Boop, Mary Poppins, Queen Elizabeth, the Grinch, Darth Vader, past presidents.
- **Fatigues:** servicemen and -women, Army, desert storm, WWI, WWII, Iraq, platoon pants, camo.

- **Feathered boas:** snake boa, fluffy Las Vegas boa, varied colors of boas, feathered fans, 20-foot never-ending boa (one end stays backstage so the audience gets the impression of endlessness), feathered wrap.

- **Fluorescent items:** glow-in-the-dark gloves, white socks, painted faces, shirts, signs. Black lights are needed to be effective.

- **Garters:** arm garters for barbershop style, on head with feathers for 1920s style, leg garters for female can-can dancers.

- **Glasses:** nerd look, professor-type glasses, cat glasses, sunglasses, movie star glasses, opera glasses, Blues Brothers glasses, spectacles, reading glasses, goggles, oversized eyeglasses, monocles.

- **Gloves:** long gloves, short gloves, two-toned gloves, fingerless, baseball, Michael Jackson single sparkly white, fluorescent for black light, military gloves, mittens.

- **Hair accessories:** barrettes, headbands, feathers, large bows, Mickey Mouse ears, antlers, cat ears.

- **Hats:** baseball cap, bridal veil, top hat, bowler (derby), fedora, barbershop skimmer, flapper headpiece, feather, sailor, cowboy hat, sun hat, visor, fruit *à la* Carmen Miranda, pirate, bandanna, beret, football helmet, hard hat, motorcycle helmet, tiara, headband, showgirl headpiece.

- **Jackets:** tux, pea coat, Judy Garland style on the girls, letter jacket, hoodie, pink ladies '50s-style jacket, clown, bolero, motorcycle, military, leather jacket, zoot suit, police, sailor white.

- **Jewelry:** earrings, bracelets, Egyptian armbands, choker, large "diamond" rings, pearl necklaces, beads.

- **Ladies skirts:** circle skirt, long skirt, wraparound, can-can, fringe, mini, grass, strips of material for Bollywood style, plastic for '60s, maxi for '70s, hoop skirt for Southern belle.

- **Novelty items:** clown nose, wings, mask, lion tail, bunny ears, cape, grass skirt, coconut bra, chaps, toga, magic wand, cane, candles, leg warmers, cell phones.

- **Robes:** choir, bath, movie star, athletic, boxing, judge, graduation, ceremonial robe, monk robe.

- **Sashes or belts:** various colors, gold or silver, chains, cowboy belt buckle, Santa, hip hugger, pirate, Michael Jackson belt, military sashes, royalty sashes, pageant sashes.

- **Shirts:** plaid with tied shirt tails for a country look, Hawaiian, patriotic, various bright colors, pastel colors, black and white, fringe for '60s look, football or baseball jersey, animal print, military, street, sailor.

- **Shoes:** character shoes, boots, go-go boots, high-topped sneakers, tap shoes, ballet point shoes, clown shoes, spats, red glitter Dorothy shoes, sandals, army, glass slippers, pumps, cowboy boots, roller skates, Heelys, house slippers, wedges.

- **Sleeves:** ruffles for Latin, torn off, fur at the bottom for a rich look, huge puffed sleeves for a small child, fringe, bell sleeves, '70s-type sleeves.

- **Spats:** white for 1920s-style shoes, penguins, go-go boots.

- **Suspenders:** elegant, clown, fireman, glitter, plaid, German lederhosen.

- **Ties:** bow ties, long ties, clown ties, skinny ties, ascots, cowboy bolo ties, clip-on, bandannas, scarves.

- **Tights:** rhinestones, fishnet, footless, opaque, colored, seamed or unseamed, white (nurse), glitter.

- **Vests:** reversible, Velcro on the lapel for quick changes, two-toned, fringe, cowboy, barbershop, fleece, orange safety, sweater, double-breasted.

- **Wigs and hairpieces:** beards, barbershop mustaches, Elvis sideburns, wigs that change color, extensions, Princess Leia braids, Dorothy pigtails, coneheads, ponytails (high or low or on the side), *Simpsons* hairdos.

- **Winter wear:** coats, gloves, scarves, snow boots, fur muffs, earmuffs, sweaters, turtlenecks, facemasks.

COSTUME CONSIDERATION

MAKE A PLAN FOR SELECTING COSTUMES

If the school is buying costumes for the ensemble, the director should select an outfit that works for all involved and that reflects school policy. If outfits are passed down year to year, costumes need to be well made, with quality material that can be easily altered and is sweat-absorbent, and in a classic style that will last over multiple years. Asking students for input is risky as they tend to think of their own preferences and what looks best on them individually. Remember—this is a costume for stage, not clothing to be worn at prom, a night on the town, or even for Sunday best.

If students are buying and keeping the costumes, choose a core group to help select the outfit(s). The director should select the panel including the director, choreographer, a few student performers, a person from the community involved in fashion, and the lighting designer. If the director wants additional students to have input, provide a costume questionnaire. The director could post a few pictures of possible outfits on a website or tape photos on the classroom door. Students can either vote by e-mail or cast a ballot in a box on the teacher's desk. This enables students to check out the choices at their convenience and not take rehearsal time.

If a committee is used to select a costume, send a complimentary ticket to an upcoming event and an autographed photo of the performers (in costume) to each member of the committee with a handwritten thank-you note. This gesture can be another source of good public relations.

TWELVE POINTS TO CONSIDER WHEN SELECTING COSTUMES

1) Costumes need to be comfortable and loose enough to allow movement. It is better to order performance wear on the larger size as it is easier to take in garments than to let out seams.

2) Stage lights will change the color and look of the clothing on stage.

3) Climate makes a difference for performers. If your ensemble rehearses in a space that isn't air-conditioned, don't opt for long sleeves, turtlenecks, dark colors, or layers.

4) Make sure the material is flattering for all body shapes and sizes.

5) Since the audience views the ensemble as one unit and not individually, hemlines equidistant from the floor work best with girls who are similar in height. If the ensemble has extremes in sizes, measuring skirts from the floor won't be effective. Instead, measure in inches from the individual's kneecap.

6) Remember that sight lines are different for each audience member. If audience seating is lower than the stage, dress lengths will appear a few inches shorter than they truly are. If part of the audience is seated in a balcony, consider raising necklines.

7) The combo, alternates, tech crew, and accompanist need to be costumed if they are a part of the show. Be inclusive when ordering.

8) Age-appropriate costumes will keep administration, parents, and audience members content.

9) The sooner the order is placed, the more likely you'll receive it in a timely fashion.

10) Affordability is important and necessary to consider.

11) The costume must fit with the style of music and choreography. Plan accordingly.

12) Costumes are meant to be seen from a distance and not up close. Don't sweat it!

SOME COSTUME BUSINESSES I'VE USED AND RECOMMEND:

▶ **Gail McInnis Productions**. Gail McInnis, *gailmproductions.com*, Hattiesburg, MS

▶ **Rivars**. Beth Rivar Slusher, *rivars.com*, Albany, IN

▶ **Satin Stitches**. Deborah Nelson, *satinstitches.com*, Minneapolis, MN

▶ **Southeastern Performance Apparel**. *sepapparel.com*, Dothan, AL

▶ **Max-Elements**. *max-elements.com*, Indianapolis, IN

▶ **Sequin City Inc**. *sequincity.com*, West New York, NJ

▶ **Mode Productions**. David Moellenkamp, *modeproductions1@yahoo.com*, Los Angeles, CA

▶ **Art Stone**. *artstonecostumes.com*, New York, NY

Retail stores, dancewear companies, bridal shops, tux shops, and formalwear outlets are other sources for costumes.

TAKIN' CARE OF BUSINESS

Ask students to sign a costume contract stating they understand that costumes must be cleaned prior to return, and in good condition with a normal amount of wear and tear. Performers will wear their costumes only on stage. No wrinkled costumes allowed on stage. An example contract is included below.

ENSEMBLE CONTRACT

Costumes are worn only during performance. There will be a $100.00 deposit due for costume "rental" for the school year. The deposit will be returned at the end of year when all costumes are returned and they have been checked to be in good condition. **Care for the costume(s) as if you personally paid for each outfit and item.**

All performers are required to have garment bags for travel and for all home shows. Please bring a clear, oversized tub with your name on it to hold shoes, props, extra costume pieces, extra tights, socks, etc.

A costume that is forgotten, misplaced, or left on the floor will automatically cause a $10.00 deduction from your deposit.

Please do not use safety pins or duct tape with the costumes. If you have any alteration concerns, you may speak to Mrs. Mack. If costumes go on stage wrinkled, pinned, or duct-taped, or with any unprofessional look, another deduction will take place, depending on the severity of the "wardrobe crime."

Any costumes repairs (such as zippers replaced, pants hemmed, buttons restitched) are your responsibility and must be taken care of before performances. Any major wardrobe malfunction should be reported to Mrs. Mack and the wardrobe mistress. Every item must have your assigned number. Personal items must be clearly marked with your name on the inside of the item.

Headliner Ladies are required to provide stage makeup, spanks, and two pairs of hose (no runs), and are expected to wear the appropriate undergarments for all performances. Headliner Men are required to provide stage makeup, a black T-shirt, a bow tie, and black socks. Black dance shoes are provided but must be polished. Students will be responsible for replacing lost or ruined shoes.

Costumes must be kept clean and pressed. Check with Mrs. Mack before laundering or dry cleaning. Certain types of sequins can be damaged if dry-cleaned. Stains, spots, and wrinkles should never be seen onstage. Costumes should smell fresh and look new. Every article of clothing has its own hanger and should be marked with your number. Be respectful in all dealings with costumes and those helping with costuming.

By signing this form, I, _____, understand the above statements and agree to uphold them throughout this Headliner academic year. I, _____,
fully understand the consequences if I do not follow these rules and regulations set forth by my instructor and department.

Signature_____ Date_____

Continuing the Tradition of Shawnee Press Excellence

Copyright © 2011 by HAL LEONARD CORPORATION
International Copyright Secured   All Rights Reserved
This page may be reproduced.

STAGE MAKEUP

Show choir is an expressive art. In communication, the eyes and the mouth are used almost exclusively to share the message. If those facial features aren't visible to the audience, you've decreased your chance of being understood. Facial features need to be enhanced to be

> The proximity of the crowd, stage size, intensity of the overhead lights, costume colors, and formal or informal nature of the show are just a few of the variables to consider before applying makeup.

seen. Applying stage makeup is different from applying everyday makeup. The proximity of the crowd, stage size, intensity of the overhead lights, costume colors, and formal or informal nature of the show are just a few of the variables to consider before applying makeup.

Male performers should use makeup only under bright stage lights and if the audience is at a distance. Apply men's makeup carefully so it presents a healthy, natural look onstage. Men may wear dark eyeliner and brick-colored blush, but they should never wear lipstick or eye color onstage.

A MAKEUP CHECK-OFF LIST
Foundation
1) Start with clean skin.
2) Apply even foundation (matching skin tones) over face and neck.
3) Blush the apple of cheeks and up near hairline. Mix powdered blush with loose powder to create a blended look.
4) Add a little blush on nose, chin, and forehead for a healthy glow.

Eyes

1) Use an eye brush to evenly distribute a pale color over the entire eyelid.
2) Using a dark color, brush powder above eyelid and on the edge of eye in a ">" pattern.
3) Add a thin line of white highlight below the eyebrow and on the inside corner of the eyelid.
4) Fill in eyebrows with a matching eyebrow pencil.
5) Use black pencil or liquid eyeliner below the eyelid and on top of the eyelid, getting right at the base of the lashes. Angle the point for a heavier look.
6) Apply mascara on top and bottom lashes. If a dramatic look is desired, use false eyelashes.

Lips
1) Heart-shape lips with darker liner. Match lip liner with lipstick and evenly fill in. Lipstick smears. Fill in slowly! Blot, reapply, and blot one more time for a longer-lasting color. To remove excess lipstick, pucker lips, insert index finger between lips, and pull out slowly.
2) Apply gloss when finished.
3) Reapply color and gloss often so it appears fresh. Lipstick and blush will soak into skin and need to be reapplied.

Powder

1) When finished, powder the entire face to even the tone and set the face.

2) Use bronzer blush to create definition. Use on shoulders, cheeks, and décolletage.

3) If the performer is sweating profusely and/or has a "glowing" face, reapply powder to reset the makeup. This may need to happen several times during the run of a show.

Remember, you are applying makeup for stage. You see yourself at a close range, but the audience will view you at a distance. If the eyes and mouth can't be seen, you will fade into the crowd. Blondes may need to apply even more or use darker shades.

TO STYLE OR NOT TO STYLE (HAIR)?

A popular pop singer reportedly insists on a clause in her backup dancers' contracts stating that the dancers' hairstyles will differ from the star's hairstyle. If the artist's tresses are down, the other performers must wear their hair up, and vice versa. I'm guessing hair color and a multitude of other stylistic details are also mentioned. Since the goal of the educator is to promote uniformity in the ensemble and to prevent star treatment, most of us don't have to worry about adding this section in any of our syllabi or lesson plans.

The eyes are the windows to the soul. The eyes must be visible to display any type of emotion or animation. If a hairstyle covers the face or if stage lights cast shadows because of hair placement, expressions won't be visible to the audience. All that rehearsal of facial choreography and expressive singing will be in vain.

As music and choreography have changed through time, so have hairstyles. If you're doing a piece from *Phantom of the Opera* and the ladies are outfitted in ball gowns, it doesn't make sense to have this elegant look topped off with pigtails, and an '80s medley wouldn't be complete without the big hair from that time period. Often directors are so busy preparing the score and working on the other details that thinking about the detail of styling hair literally puts them over the edge.

The solution? Ask a male and a female student to be the "hair chairs." The students will become part of the creative process and thus gain more ownership in the program. The "hair chair" can use a check-off sheet a few days before each performance. The males in the group should have a clean-cut look with hair just touching ears and collar. If the hair is long, the student must put it in a ponytail. In my student/performer contracts, I ask the males to wear their hair short. Personally, I like the look of long hair on males, but in performances I don't want the males and females to have mistaken identities on stage. The audience shouldn't fail to differentiate gender in any shape or form. Males can change their hairstyles once they are not a part of the "performing team." I carefully approach this subject and am not confrontational but, rather, simply matter-of-fact. It is a show choir stage rule and if the students want to perform, they will follow and respect the rules.

Men must have haircuts that keep the eyes uncovered; be clean shaven; and have a hair color or style that wouldn't draw unwanted or negative attention on stage. No piercings or tattoos may be visible during performance. My students know they can look any way they want on the street, but when they are performing, the "Disney" standard is utilized. All performers must appear well-groomed, clean-cut, and all-American. The all-American definition is rapidly changing. However, many of our audience members still appreciate the old-school values and will be more supportive of the program if they can relate to the look on the stage.

Females should use bobby pins or clips that are not visible to the audience. Colored barrettes, bows, or headbands are used only if part of a costume. If hair is parted, females should part it on the same side. Hair swept up shows a lovely silhouette of neck, nape, and shoulders. Wigs and hairpieces can quickly change the look. However, nothing is more unnerving to an audience than to  see hairpieces flying off girls' heads. Pin securely, and then pin again! And ladies—please, no hair glitter!

DETAILS

What is the difference between a true professional and an aspiring performer? Attention to detail. Novice show choir members might not have believed that their exact stage position mattered until they realized that the pyrotechnic flash pot was located right under their feet.

> What is the difference between a true professional and an aspiring performer? Attention to detail.

Often, a choreographer will demonstrate a move without specifying the exact angle the arms are held, whether the head is tilted to the right or left, or if the toes are pointed or flexed. It would take forever to describe each and every position of the body. Students need to get in the habit of listening with all their senses. Instead of asking questions, train students to watch and see if they can figure it out themselves. It will be a much more valuable lesson. Getting all the details is important in every line of work. Learn this life lesson now; it could make a difference with a grade, a job, or maybe even a relationship.

One of my favorite stories about details took place during my sophomore year in college, when I enrolled in a chemistry class. I had heard from upperclassmen that this popular class would fill quickly. The professor, Dr. Pickerell (known by his students as simply "Pick"), was notorious for his eccentric and sometimes outlandish teaching style. Even though it was a required course and there would be lots of homework, I still looked forward to the class.

The first day I rushed to get a front-row seat but ended up in the back, because the front section was filled with eager chemistry majors. In strolled Pick, in a plaid blazer, striped pants, and the biggest pair of horn-rimmed glasses I'd ever seen. No one even blinked; he fit the bill of the genius professor and mad scientist all rolled into one. Pick sauntered to the center of the room, where there was a table full of test tubes, all containing liquids of various colors and amounts.

Pick selected one of the test tubes and held it in the air so everyone could observe. He explained that by tasting the liquid, true scholars would be able to analyze and identify the taste—especially those who really paid close attention to the experiment. Pick proceeded to stick his finger in the solution, then licked off his finger and passed the small container down the front row.

Each student bravely stuck his or her finger in the test tube and cautiously sampled the solution. One by one, the chemistry majors passed the container down the row, making faces as they cleaned off their index fingers.

Pick then proceeded to tell the class that this substance was … urine! He wanted us to learn the importance of attention to details. If we had paid attention and noticed the smallest of details, we would have observed that he stuck his index finger into the liquid but he then licked off his ring finger. I will never forget that lesson in details and paying close attention. I'm also thankful that I didn't end up in the front row.

I'M JUST SAYING...

Early in my teaching career, a student framed a quote for me, and I am reminded of the importance of the message each time I walk by. "Countless, unseen details are often the only difference between mediocre and magnificent." Details can truly make a difference; just ask those students who sat in the front row of Pick's chemistry class. ☺

> "Countless, unseen details are often the only difference between mediocre and magnificent."

CHAPTER 6:
ON WITH THE SHOW

SETTING THE STAGE

Setting the stage for a show happens long before performers set foot onstage. A great performance needs to start with a great first impression. An audience member's first call to the box office for reservations can have a positive or negative influence long before he or she arrives at the show. Phone recordings and/or Internet ticket information should provide accurate show dates, show times, performance location and pertinent information about the upcoming performance(s). Phone or e-mail responses need to be professional and courteous, as a well-mannered reply can build anticipation for the upcoming event.

If the show will take place in a theater with **limited parking**, ask the performers to save the best parking for the patrons. Do everything possible to make the evening successful from the start. This little detail can get everyone started on the right foot; and if audience members are parking closer, their feet won't be tired from walking long distances.

Ushers need to look professional and be prepared. Besides the obvious job of directing people to their seats and distributing programs, ushers should be familiar with seating charts, cry rooms, ticket information, refund policies, and recording rules. They must be able to direct people to the restrooms, refreshments, and, in an emergency, shelter or safety. Ushers need to be pleasant and positive about the show. If they have previously seen the show, they need to be cautious about making any judgments or sharing program information, thus ruining any special effects or taking away the *magic* of the performance.

Once the house is opened, **keep the stage clear**. If performers are still rehearsing, tuning instruments, decorating the stage, or walking onstage in costume, the enchantment and thrill of the theater disappears. Audience members will have difficulty separating the rehearsal from the actual show.

Set the stage with preshow music. Ask the sound engineer to play musical excerpts that set up the show. If the theme is about dance, use dance selections that aren't being performed but that will prepare the audience for what is to come musically. If the goal is to get the audience revved up for the show, play lively tunes that lead right up to the opening note, rather than tranquil and soothing music.

Stage decorations can range from simple to elaborate. If your concert will take place in the fall, line the lip of the stage with pumpkins and autumn colors. Or better yet, sponsor a jack-o'-lantern contest and award the winner a homemade pumpkin pie. If it's a winter or Christmas concert, adorn the stage with artificial trees trimmed with ornaments and twinkly lights. Posters, artwork, fabric, flags, ladders, large boxes, antique trunks, rope lights, and helium-filled balloons are other effective and easy-to-find decorations. If you're using latex balloons, check that there are no latex allergies among your performers or helpers. Poinsettias, mums, and green plants add a simple elegance to the stage. Even better, use the plants as a special thank-you to be given away at the end of the concert.

I'M JUST SAYING...

"All the world's a stage," suggests William Shakespeare. We are always performing, whether onstage or off. In other words, the show doesn't begin at the downbeat. Someone is always watching you.

> People may forget what you said and did, but they will always remember how you made them feel.

STAGE FRIGHT

Surprisingly, students and professionals continue to suffer from stage fright. It seems strange to me that opening-night nerves would even be an issue in today's world. Young people are performing and auditioning more than ever. They are being recorded by friend's cell phones, flip cameras, video surveillance cameras, school monitors, Skype, and who knows what else. In fact, students today have very little—if any—privacy. Students are also auditioning for reality television competitions, talent contests, music videos, and dance competitions, and posting YouTube videos to an almost dangerous degree. And yet with all this auditioning, the symptoms or extents of stage fright haven't decreased over the years.

In my early college years, I went through a time of being overly nervous about the thought of performing in front of people. I knew I had to get over those feelings since my goal of being an educator meant I would be "performing" in front of people the rest of my life. I had to get to the bottom of my fears and face them before I allowed my stage fright to get in the way of a major decision.

That semester, one of my college English composition instructors assigned a research paper on a subject of our choosing. I opted for "stage fright" and immediately started interviewing a variety of "performers" in various stages of life. I interrogated everyone from the reigning Miss Kansas (who had just won a talent award at the Miss America pageant), to radio DJs, TV personalities, Broadway performers, area sports celebrities, college presidents, cruise ship performers, and even some local politicians. I covered the gamut.

As I researched the topic at the library (that was in the days when we actually had to *walk* over to the library and physically select and carry books to check out), I found out some amazing information that instantly helped. I realized that everyone suffered with some type of stage fright. In fact, if you didn't get a little adrenaline flowing through the body, the performance wouldn't have that needed edge.

The best part of writing the research paper was hearing what remedies the performers used. Even though the interviews took place years ago, the solutions are still quite valid today. Stage fright is synonymous with self-consciousness or being unprepared. That is easy to fix, right? Perfect practice makes perfect performance. You must practice performing. Videotape the performance and then analyze. Repeat this several times until it is second nature to the performers. This method really works.

> Perfect practice makes perfect performance. You must practice performing.

Keep in mind that the audience wants you to succeed. Slow down your breathing and find a place to fix your eyes: maybe not staring directly into someone else's eyes but above the eyebrows. Take a moment and think what you are doing before you begin. Practice performing—the more you perform, the easier it becomes. When you feel that surge of nervous energy coming on (butterflies in the stomach, dry throat, clamminess in the hands, shortness of breath), let it happen and ride it through. Tell yourself you'll get through, you've been through worse. Fear heightens energy and adds a sparkle to the eyes and color to the cheeks. Remember, nobody ever died from stage fright! And if none of these remedies works? *Picture the entire audience in underwear, 3-D glasses, and propeller beanie hats.*

STAGE MOMS

No one is brave (or brainless?) enough to write a chapter on stage moms. No one, that is, but a genuine, true, scars-to-show-and-prove stage mom. I wear my badge proudly. I admit, however (and not with pride), that I have probably done some silly things as a stage mom. If I have ever said or done anything as a pushy stage mom or exhibited any rude behavior to any of you unbeknownst, I, "Mama Rose" Mack, sincerely apologize. Years ago, *Peanuts* cartoonist Charles M. Schulz said that a good education is the next best thing to a pushy mother. I think Mr. Schulz would be quite disturbed to see today's stage moms in action.

Seriously, I am concerned about the need to include this chapter. Having been in the dance and music world as a teacher and adjudicator, and now being on the other side of the table with a daughter in competitive dance and a son in Little League baseball and other youth sports, I am not thrilled about some of the things I see and hear. John Q Public needs to stand up to stage moms—and to helicopter parents, the ones hovering over their children right now as the children need to make some mistakes on their own. How will children learn to grow if they are never allowed to make mistakes or fall down? Kids of all ages need to learn about failure—and not just read about it from a text. Parents, teach your children to work for something and not to succumb to the immediate gratification trap.

> **Parents, teach your children to work for something and not to succumb to the immediate gratification trap.**

How do you deal with stage moms? First of all we must accept that everyone—even the mother from "H-E-double-hockey-sticks"—was put in front of us for a reason. We may see that reason in this lifetime, or maybe we will never know. Whatever reason, the stage mom is a part of your program and you must have a constructive way of dealing with her and the situations that arise.

Need some good ideas regarding dealing with difficult parents? Like a cancer, negativity spreads rapidly. It needs to be cut out before it continues to grow. Blast beautiful music with positive lyrics from your speakers, hang up inspirational posters for parents to read as they wait, put curtains along the windows to discourage negative commentary. Take out chairs from the waiting room, hallway, or in your office. This may seem over the top, but at the dance studio where I teach, we even offer coffee in to-go cups and encourage a walk and talk group (away from the studio). I keep a candle burning (homemade apple pie scent) in my office. Who feels like acting ugly or being a jerk when being reminded of Mom and Grandma?

I'M JUST SAYING...

I'll just mention a few horror (and yet totally true!) stories from my real-life judging situations. Some "low-lights" from the past: the parents who bought Miracle-Ear hearing aids so they could hear the judges' critiques before getting the score sheets; the time Mac Huff and I had to have police escorts down the elevator at a highly competitive show choir competition; watching a teacher throw a rather large trophy in the fountain at Epcot (because the group came in second and not first); the winning group's tires that were slashed in the parking lot; and the young children who were "paid" to take photos of the judges' critique sheets to prove that the judges erased scores. (Heck, yes, we erase! We are music educators, not math majors. You try adding up 25 scores while talking into a tape recorder and writing comments on a separate score sheet. Hmmph!) And don't think we don't see you not applauding for any group but your own. Talk about lack of sportsmanship! What are you teaching your children?

My desire is to write one last book full of "silver box" stories—about ordinary people doing kind things and using encouraging words. Appreciate the people around you and don't forget to say thank you. We deserve and need to hear more of these tales. Go out and change the world. You can make a difference!

Stage moms—use your energy in a positive and productive manner. Help your own child by helping the ensemble, the instructor, the department, the school, the community, and the world. Stage moms—push only when invited!

> **Stage moms—use your energy in a positive and productive manner.**

CALLING ALL MEN

Choral programs, it seems, either have a considerable male following or they don't. Some causes might include the presence of feeder programs, the strength of the athletic programs, the existence of other fine arts organizations, the size and location of the school, and the traditions of music in the community. Some of this is beyond your control. But you can do some definite things to make a difference in participation.

One of the easiest ways to recruit men for your choral program is to let them see other men being successful and having fun onstage. This is a time that the show choir can recruit for the rest of the choral department and the fine arts in general. Present a *really good* (that is the key) show choir. Be sure the performers are confident and love what they are doing. We sometimes forget the cleverness of our younger audiences. If the show doesn't grab the attention of the audience and make them want to participate, instead of *recruiting* males you will have accomplished just the opposite. If you don't have a group that is ready to go out, bring in a local college ensemble or locate a professional touring company. If you don't have the budget to bring in the talent, take your students to the talent. If students can't afford to travel or buy the tickets, figure out a way to get them there. Bring in "cool" alums to talk to younger guys or ensembles. If you can get a nucleus of top-notch males, eager to perform, you can grow your entire program.

When I first started teaching, I was so excited about music and getting to teach that I didn't have a problem of recruitment but a problem of sharing my vision. Being in the middle of south-central Kansas, many of my students came from area farming towns and smaller communities that hadn't experienced live musical theater. The only type of barbershop they were familiar with was the one on the corner that offered men's haircuts.

But the community was supportive and willing to believe with me. To get started, I accompanied four male singers to the closest regional theater to see the show *Forever Plaid*. The guys were fired up and had a clear mental image of the success that would follow four guys singing close harmonies, having a blast on stage.

Caution: Your administration may say that your library has plenty of performance videos. Tech-savvy members of the administration may suggest that students check out YouTube videos on the antiquated computer in your office. If that's the case, take your principal, superintendent, and board president with you to a live performance. Again, be sure it is a program that you want to emulate. Nothing in the world replaces live theater: feeling the buzz in the audience before the curtains open, getting autographs and meeting the performers after the show, and the thrill and excitement as the audience leaps for a standing ovation. The live reaction can't be duplicated on film or on YouTube.

Teachers, if you want to share students or have good relationships with other instructors and administrators, you must remember to play fair and "share." Word gets around about what is said in the teachers' lounge. Just a word of advice—it takes a village to recruit a male. You'd better have a village standing behind you. That means there'll be some give and take with your time, talents and students. No ifs, ands, or buts (or butts!). In the end, it will be a win-win situation for you, the student, and everyone involved.

I'M JUST SAYING...

And if the above doesn't bring results, call all the men. Talk to them personally. Don't text, e-mail, Facebook, or put up posters expecting them to flock to your classroom. Talk to them personally and individually. Does it take more work? Yes! But it will build your program from the bass clef up!

MAINTAINING MEN IN MUSIC

First you must recruit the men and then you must work on retention. In the movie *Field of Dreams*, we hear "build it and they will come." Build your program by choosing quality men's literature. So many great compositions and arrangements are out there. It would be silly of me to list just a few, as I would be sure to leave out someone's favorite—plus, it would take pages and pages to list all of the compositions. Even if you don't have a men's ensemble, choose one number for the men in your group in which they can be successful. Before they perform for the rest of the class, secretly talk to the ladies in the ensemble and ask them to be encouraging

with their faces and response. Explain how they can take a role in recruiting and retaining the men in the department by being encouraging—not phony or fake but genuinely supportive with their facial and verbal expressions.

The first day of class, provide an activity that shows how physically challenging the course will be. This activity (music) is not for the weak at heart. We all want the same budget and perks that the athletic department has; treat your students like athletes. To this day I can do as many—if not more—pushups than most of the males in my dance and music classes (thanks to my yoga teacher, Miss Renee). My hope is that the students see that I am willing to put in the extra effort and am totally committed to the ensemble. I want them to see that I'm not afraid of hard work and that I will work right along beside them. Challenge them with an activity that will push them out of their comfort zone.

A big brother/big sister program is another effective way to keep men involved in the choir. Assign an older brother to an incoming male. The big brother can check up on his little bro' outside of class. All students need connections in order to stay linked together. Often, with demanding teaching schedules, the teacher doesn't have time and, frankly, the teachers aren't as cool as the older guys. This can work when it is time for contest, performances, tours, or exams, as well as for absenteeism and tardiness. The big brother can ensure that his little brother is there on time, has the right costume, and knows what is going on. This saves the teacher precious time in answering the same question repeatedly and from making hundreds of phone calls, texts, or e-mails.

Insist that your males look strong on stage. The women in the ensemble must stand, walk, and dance in a feminine manner. Nigel Lythgoe, executive producer of *So You Think You Can Dance*, says that dancing is role playing and that a guy must look stronger than the girl he is dancing with. Ask your guys to dance the part they are given.

If you have members who are involved in sports, go cheer on the team. Then, in class Monday morning, throw out a positive comment about the game. Show that you genuinely care.

> **Attend activities the guys are involved in outside of class.**

I'M JUST SAYING...

> *The best way to recruit and keep guys involved in your program? Feed them! Feeding their souls with quality music is one way but another good tactic is to feed them, period. Homemade cookies on a special day can make a big impact and keep them coming back for more.*

COMPETITION

Like a good politician, I could be swayed to vote "yea" or "nay" on the issue of competition. It's not that I am indecisive on the subject matter of competing. I've witnessed and been a part of some top-notch, well-run competitions that were positive experiences for all involved. I've also seen great show choirs walk away from an event with their tails between their legs, lower lips on the ground, and tears running down their cheeks as they loaded the bus to go home.

So I'll take the easy way out and say, I do think competition is what keeps some directors and schools ticking, good or bad. It is a fact that if a prize is given at the end of a race, the runner will work harder than if there isn't a prize at all. The directors get a natural high, as do their students, from the thrill of the hunt. First, they must find the perfect show, costumes, choreographer, soloist, set, and competition venue, and it goes on and on.

The competition keeps them keen and on the cutting edge. It's how directors recruit and keep students coming back year after year: They are training students to go out and continue the competition tradition. As long as the director, students, administration, and—most important—the parents can keep it in perspective, I say ... let the games begin.

> **Competitions can be good incentives to rehearse and improve.**

Before any event, study the critique sheet. It helps to know what the judges are evaluating. Don't gripe about how unfair the judging is if you haven't done your homework. If the score sheet is weighted heavily on vocals and you have a highly choreographed ballad that your students can barely sing, don't blame the judges. Focus on the learning part. Students and parents will react exactly as you allow them to. They will watch you (the fearless leader) and how you take it all in. Be careful! It is not always what you say but what you don't say.

The tiniest detail can put one ensemble in front of another on a score sheet. Do your best to think through every area of the show, how it fits together, and what you can improve. Normally, it is the program that is being adjudicated. Don't take it out on the singers. They are doing what you, the director, told them to do.

Of course, a lot also depends on the panel of adjudicators. Don't try to second-guess what the panel wants or copy last year's winning formula. Do what you do best and then hope for the best. If it doesn't go your way, leave knowing that you did everything you could to make the day a success but that it just wasn't your day with that set of subjective opinions. Which is better: apples, oranges, or kiwis? Ask ten people and you'll see how complicated the decision making becomes.

For others, a successful format could be a festival instead of a competition. Everything that takes place at a competition also takes place at a festival, minus the trophies. Students still get the opportunity to see other groups perform, to work with professional music and dance educators, and to spend time with other show choir and jazz musicians. At the end of the event, all the choirs come together to perform a massed number. The difference is that every group goes back to its school in a more even-keeled manner. You don't have the big ups and downs that you do in the competition circuit. The downside is that your students won't work as hard if a trophy or rating and ranking aren't involved. Thank you, athletic programs! Good or bad, that is how the world operates, and good luck trying to reprogram the competitive nature of our youth (and the even more competitive nature of the parents). Don't lose sight of the goal: motivating students to the highest degree of excellent performance.

ADJUDICATION NOTES

The following comments and suggestions about adjudicating a choral event are beneficial for people who are interested in choral adjudication and for instructors preparing for competition. It might be helpful to read the list to ensemble members and their families before competing. This list will give insight into some of the qualifications necessary for the judging panel and some of the things judges are responsible for besides scoring.

Judging is much harder than it looks. If you don't believe me, set up your own mock competition using past choral performances. Hand out mock adjudication sheets and run fifteen to twenty video performances back to back, without a break. This activity is educational and tricky, and, most important, will silence anyone who thinks otherwise.

As a successful adjudicator, you should:
1) Embrace the score sheet in front of you. It doesn't matter if you used so-and-so's score sheet last week and liked it better. You are hired to use this new score sheet. Be professional and stick to the given sheet.

2) Nurture the students instead of tearing them down with negative and unconstructive comments. Time is of essence, but don't fill it with negativity. Rather, sandwich your comments. First, comment on something the ensemble does well, then place a critique in the middle, and end with something positive. This is the way to ensure that students and directors will "hear" your comments and critiques.

3) Do critiques in the time given. Don't miss the opening of the next ensemble's performance because you're still writing comments about the previous group.

4) Make a decision and don't change your opinion.

5) Focus on the entire show and not just one aspect of the performance.

6) Maintain numerical consistency. Don't allow yourself to be influenced by fatigue, audience applause, other judges' comments or expressions, time of day, lack of sleep, etc.

7) Be consistent with score and taped comments. The two need to match up. A good adjudicator can back up his or her scores with the written or taped critique.

8) Relate an adequate amount of information on how to improve before the next performance— whether that be finals or the next competition or home show.

9) Work with the score sheet throughout time and analyze decisions through time.

10) Note specific occurrences on the score sheet.

11) Reread the score sheet to make sure it is intelligible to the reader.

12) Be clear in all communication. Be specific in comments rather than merely saying, "You all need to improve." That type of vague comment doesn't help the ensemble get any better and is confusing in the context.

13) Avoid fatigue and boredom. The adjudicator should feel as fresh for the final group as he/ she does for the very first performance of the day. In the middle of the set, one needs to be alert and not get distracted or bored.

14) Steer clear of anger. Maybe you've suggested to a competing choir that it make changes in the ballad and the ensemble is still singing the same material the same way. Don't get angry, as you are not aware of everything concerning the ensemble and possible reasons for the choices.

15) Trust the judging system. It will work if you are serious and do a good job in your scoring.

16) Never single out one student on the tape or in writing. This will make others in the ensemble feel bad. Do so only in private, after discussion with the instructor.

17) Never listen to the other judges. Stand up for what you believe in; you were hired to do a job coming from your own expertise and background

18) Act professional on and off the judging panel.

19) Never let the audience applause or lack of enthusiasm affect the score.

20) Always place the student first.

I'M JUST SAYING...

Competition can be a rewarding experience. It is important to take the above guidelines seriously. It is also helpful to be on both sides of the panel. In doing so, one will understand the vast impact that another person's comments can make on the ensemble. And above all, remember that adjudicators, tabulators, directors, and students are all human. Do your best, and then remember that it is just one person's opinion. Another day, another outcome.

TRAGEDY TOMORROW

When I was asked to write this resource book for music educators, the editors at Shawnee Press suggested it would be fun to sprinkle some humorous personal stories throughout the book. I've realized that I've been so serious in spitting out information that I haven't done much sprinkling. So I'll share a couple of my favorite show choir stories. The names and places haven't been changed but I don't think those people will ever read the book. If they do, I'll apologize later. If you don't feel like smiling, turn a few pages. You won't miss anything educational if you skip this section of the book.

There's nothing educational about humor—except that I've been researching exceptional teachers, and guess what they all share in their teaching: Master teachers use humor and laughter in the classroom. Laughter triggers healthy physical changes in the body and it bands people together. When you laugh, your brain's chemistry changes and everything works better. A powerful antidote to stress, humor is infectious. And best of all—it's free and can be shared at any time and with anyone. Feeling stressed? Read on…

A lesson in communication—not sure who got the lesson!
One of my favorite communication (or lack-of-communication) stories took place when I tried to explain to my 85-year-old grandfather what I did for a living. My grandfather was Southern Baptist and so, to be safe, I used the word "choreographer" rather than dance instructor. I explained that I even had videotapes of my choreography and that the next time I visited him, I would let him see just what I did. I thought he understood until I got a call from a friend who had just left the local coffee shop. My grandfather was bragging to everyone who would listen about his granddaughter Valerie, the "pornographer." And, yes, he also told everyone that I even had my own pornography videos. Let's just say that I wasn't in a hurry to visit the coffee shop anytime soon.

The sounds of silence … and a wedding?
The year that Joel, the new Headliner accompanist and now dear friend, joined the Butler music faculty, our show choir was scheduled to do an all-school assembly at a rather large area high school. It was Joel's first time playing the school's electronic keyboard. He was proud of himself as he figured out which button to push for the organ sound. When the Headliners were in the middle of performing "Wedding Bell Blues," Joel was supposed to play "Here Comes the Bride" as the bride and groom walked down the risers. As the male soloist reached into his pocket to grab the ring, Joel pushed the wrong button and, instead of hitting the organ stop, he hit the machine gun stop. It was so realistic that the whole auditorium froze. If you could have seen the look on that bride's face! We all had a good laugh about it—much later. To this day Joel and I can't look at each other at weddings when the organ starts playing the bridal chorus.

Keep it appropriate
This is another true story with a not-so-funny lesson in humor. My dad, a music educator of 46 years, always taught me that if you offended one person when using humor in a show, you couldn't use the bit. I had carefully tried to come up with some barbershop jokes that were basic and nonoffensive. What better topic than fishing, I decided. I walked onstage and said, "Did you hear about the one-armed fisherman who caught a fish? It was this big!" and I held up my right arm and kept my left behind my back. As I said it, I noticed that a person in the front row had only one arm. I kicked myself for ignoring my dad's advice. I share that story with you because what is funny to one person may not be funny to someone else. Think before you share something that might not be suitable for every audience member.

COMEDY TONIGHT

What to pack—banana peels?

I've always tried to program one song in each show to make 'em laugh, one heartfelt ballad to make 'em cry, and one number to make 'em think on the drive home. If you can do those things every show, you are doing something right. I learned this lesson from my first dance teacher, Miss Mary, a former Rockette and a master educator. She taught me to always leave 'em wanting more. OK—maybe I haven't totally mastered that part of the lesson. I teach the way I write and pack: cramming in every little tidbit, thinking that the extras squeezed in (words/shoes) might be helpful to someone out there.

Tim Seelig, Shawnee Press author (and all-around musical genius), explains that cramming numbers into a program, book, or lesson plan is a piece of insecurity that all musicians possess. We produce longer concerts because we nervously fear the audience may not like anything we program. But if we give 'em even more, maybe there will be something they do like.

It's the same with comedy. We extend jokes and punch lines on stage, thinking that if it goes on long enough, maybe it will become funnier with each passing moment. Unfortunately, just the opposite is true. Teaching comedic timing is easier said than done. Comedic talent comes naturally to some and bypasses others. I've even gone as far as showing old VHS recordings of "classic" comedy episodes with students. I won't share that list so as not to date myself—but those old sitcoms, now *that* was humor. I do think some of the YouTube videos are pretty hilarious ("Shane sings five octaves" is a classic), but I've come to realize that humor is often very personal. Work hard to find the laughter and to use comedic talents. Slapstick (slipping on a banana peel) is still funny to all ages if done correctly.

Know for whom you are performing

This story comes from my good friend Cheri Helmer-Riensche of Omaha, Nebraska. Cheri's show choir was invited to sing at a Christmas luncheon at the University of Nebraska Medical Center. While Cheri's show choir entertained, the audience feasted on a catered Italian meal. The singers were absolutely starving, and the aroma from the Italian food permeated the room. The next day, Cheri wrote a thank-you note and teasingly said, "The next time we're invited, could you serve liver and onions or some horrible meal so the singers aren't tempted to eat with you?" Cheri received a call a couple of days later asking for an apology note. Little did she know, her show choir had been singing for the Liver Transplant Christmas luncheon. Oops!

A painful farewell

And then there was Bart. Bart was one of those special students; I never thought the two of us would survive his time at Butler. And somehow we did. The very last concert, during the final ballad, I could tell that many of the graduating students were getting emotional. I was standing behind the risers, in back of the singers, and I noticed Bart in the top back row, his hand behind his back, waving at me. I was surprised but, appreciating the sweet sentiment, I went over and took his hand until the number was over. After the concert, the choir gathered one last time and I shared the beautiful, touching moment Bart and I had experienced on the final ballad. Bart quickly quipped, "Yeah, Mrs. Mack, I didn't know what you were doing. I passed gas and was waving the fumes away when you came up and took my hand. I was as surprised as you were!" And then the choir shared tears one last time—however, this time we shared tears of joy.

MAKE 'EM LAUGH

It takes its toll

I'm telling this story especially for my friend Greg Jasperse (otherwise known as "the great jazz person"), as for some reason he thinks this story is hilarious. I don't find any humor in this story but will let you, the reader, decide. I was taking the Kansas turnpike, running late from a show choir rehearsal and hurrying to teach a tap class. I was on the phone with a vocal recruit and was driving my husband Tom's SUV, forgetting he didn't have a K-tag—meaning I should have been in a different lane to pay the 75-cent toll. It was too late: I ran through the tollgate and kind of smashed through the toll arm because the arm never lifted. A long line of cars was behind me and I couldn't back up the car. I rolled down my window, still on the phone with the recruit. I waved at the tollbooth attendant, not knowing what else to do, and yelled across, "Hi—I'm late for tap class. Thanks!" Big smile, one last wave, and I drove on through. I figured I'd get a call the next day from a person of authority. I kind of forgot about the incident as there was no damage to my husband's car and I never received a phone call from the toll people. A few months later, I shared the story with a friend (who happened to be the emcee for our spring concert). So, you guessed it, my husband heard the story from him—along with everyone else in the audience that night (bigger oops!). I now have this tollgate phobia … but no matter how big of a hurry I'm in, I always smile and wave at the tollbooth attendant and then duck—just in case!

Sword hitting the fan

I know you may be thinking I meant for something else to hit the fan. Another true story that took place in rehearsal: The Butler Headliner men were rehearsing "Into the Fire" from *The Scarlet Pimpernel*. Against my better judgment, I allowed the guys to use "real" swords for their fake fighting. The heavy swords were made out of metal but didn't have sharp-tipped edges. The swords reflected the light and clanked like real swords. As the guys were in the middle of the dance break (or sword break, as it were), Josh reached up with his sword, forgetting that the ceiling fan was on. The sword hit the fan, knocking it out of Josh's hands—into Brady's eyebrow. Brady wasn't hurt, but the sword left a little scratch above his eyebrow. I started screaming, "Get me a Diet Coke now!" I knew we didn't have ice close by and I put the can on Brady's eyebrow the same way I would have used an icepack. After it was over, the Headliners were impressed with my resourcefulness. We decided it made a great story for Brady to tell his grandkids someday. *Oh, this scar? It came from a sword fight in my show choir class.*

Sticks and stones and students

This is the last story I'll share, and again this is directly from my friend Cheri Helmer-Riensche and her first week in a new high school. Cheri has a phenomenal reputation for being a master teacher and her students all loved and adored her—all except for Antoine, a recent transfer from a nearby school. Practically a high school dropout, Antoine had trouble with authority and was a true troublemaker in every sense of the word. When Mrs. Riensche asked him to take off his hat, Antoine muttered, "Try to make me, you old witch." He used a word a little stronger than "witch," but I'll leave that to your imagination. You could have heard a pin drop as Cheri walked up to him, got right in his face with eyes ablaze, and said, "Antoine, you can call me whatever you want. You can call me ugly and fat. But don't you ever, ever, EVER call me … OLD!" This was not at all the reaction Antoine was expecting. Both he and Mrs. Riensche started laughing. That was a turning point for Antoine. From that day forward, he was Mrs. Riensche's most devoted fan and a leader for the department. Keep a sense of humor—it could save a student, seriously.

THE GAMES PEOPLE PLAY

For any choir, team, or class to work together in a positive manner, the members must be comfortable with one another. Icebreaker games can rejuvenate and energize your ensembles. *Icebreakers: 60 Fun Activities that Will Build a Better Choir!* was my first resource book based on games and activities for music educators. I successfully used these ideas in my own music classroom and they were received with such great enthusiasm that my next book, *Icebreakers 2: 64 More Games and Activities*, soon followed.

Students need a place to belong—a family away from home. The more you demonstrate to your students that you care and respect them as individuals (know their names and something about them), the more they will care and respect you and your music program. Your classroom just might be the only "home" some of your students know. In 400 B.C., Plato said, "You can discover more about a person in an hour of play than in a year of conversation." Learn about your students while everyone is having fun.

I've picked out a few games from the books mentioned above. The first game, "Silent Line Drills," is from the first *Icebreaker* book. I used this game every week with one of my middle school tap classes. When I first started teaching tap, I was frustrated at the girls who came to class five minutes late. They were texting the latest gossip in the dressing rooms. They would then come in and stand next to the same girls each week. At first I was really angry with the whole class. Then I stepped back and thought, *I've taught for years and should be a better teacher than this.* The following week I introduced "Silent Line Drills" and its variations and haven't had these problems since. Now, the girls rush to class as they don't want to miss the week's drill. By playing the line game, they end in a different lineup each week, so the little cliques vanished and I didn't have to raise my voice or start class in a negative manner. The Icebreaker took care of the problem automatically.

The question was different each week: What is your favorite fast-food item, favorite Super Bowl commercial, scariest movie, "hottest" movie star, etc. The girls—without talking—had to get in a straight line alphabetically with their answer. I would time the girls to see how fast they could get in line, and if they beat their record, they would get a treat at the end of the month. This game solved tardiness and clique issues, and helped me get to know them—all in less than a minute with a simple Icebreaker activity.

A game my son Zane invented is called "Heads up! Singer's up!" and is found in *Icebreakers 2*. This is similar to the old "Heads up! Seven up!" game elementary students play during rainy day recesses. The twist is that the students sing instead of putting their thumbs down. With students sitting in a big circle, choose seven students as the first group. The remainder of the students stay seated with heads lowered and eyes closed, and each should form a fist with thumb pointed in the air. The "chosen seven" each tap someone's thumb and then lightly sing a predetermined song into that person's ear. Students are encouraged to disguise their voices in timbre, tone, or presentation to confuse the listener. When each of the seven has performed, he or she tiptoes to the front of the room. When all have finished, the teacher says, "Heads up," and the seated students may then sit up and open their eyes. The students who had their thumbs pressed and a song sung to them will all stand and guess which classmate sang in their ears. If they guess correctly, they replace the person in the next round. If incorrect, they must sit down, and the singer gets another chance. This activity accomplishes many things including solo singing, experimenting with range, timbre, sounds, dynamics, etc. It is much harder to guess the person than you'd imagine.

I'M JUST SAYING...

As I was creating Icebreakers for the books, I would experiment with the games in class. One of the biggest flops was the day I had everyone take off their shoes and put them in the middle of the floor. They were supposed to grab different shoes and try to match up. The only problem was we tried the game on a day that all forty singer/dancers wore matching black jazz shoes. Students didn't want to touch anyone else's shoes. It took more than an hour getting eighty shoes sorted out. Oops!

IT'S ELEMENTARY (KIDS!) MY DEAR...

There are teachers who have the gift. I'm not talking about the musical gift, but the talent to work with elementary-age students. Honestly, if we want this world to be changed for the better, our best teachers should be in the elementary schools. Passionate teachers can make a huge impact on a youngster.

> **Passionate teachers can make a huge impact on a youngster.**

Surprisingly, when asked what or who shaped your life, college students frequently mention their elementary teachers—and even more specifically, their elementary music teachers.

How do you work with elementary students in a musical setting? The energy seems to be bouncing off the walls—and the students never seem to stop moving. So do they get to move twice as much on stage? The answer depends on the talent level of the elementary students, the time frame, and the goals. Normally, grade school children performing on risers should do more choralography (only mainly upper-body movements) and fewer actual dance moves. The exception to this rule is if a featured dance highlights one student. Then, depending on stage space, let the performer(s) move.

Save props for older students. It is safer and much easier not to deal with an abundance of props. If you decide to use them, tell students they are a reward. Props can be taken away from an individual or the entire class if any horseplay is involved. Students must "earn" props.

Use only encouraging words when dealing with elementary students. Even when being critical, do so in the most positive manner. Don't talk down to younger kids. They should be treated with respect. Many times they know as much about what's going on as the teacher does.

BASIC CHOREOGRAPHY TECHNIQUES FOR THE ELEMENTARY STUDENT

- Use mostly arms when adding movement. Once students have mastered that, go sparingly with the feet. Save turns and fancy footwork for the older, more mature students.

- Make use of hands to teach foot patterns when the students are ready. If the students can understand the movements and perform them with their hands, they will then be able to transfer the ideas to the feet. Try this with a front essence step (for example, "Tea for Two").

- Make up silly words to use when teaching a pattern. If the elementary students can say the pattern, they will get it into their bodies. The pattern will also help them memorize faster.

- Turning around is very confusing for the younger elementary students. Kindergartners through fourth-graders should stay focused to the front. Omit pivots and spins for younger students.

- Focus the students' energy. Middle school performers seem to have the energy zapped right out of them. Good performers are full of energy from the moment they walk on stage.

- Students of all ages pick up lessons early. Be careful what you teach.

- Teach the choreography correctly the first time. What is taught first will be what is remembered in the heat of battle. Make changes only in case of emergency.

I'M JUST SAYING...

You'll find many websites with handouts and information on ways to praise kids. In case you don't have time to search, I am including some of my favorite phrases. These phrases work if the student has truly done something that deserves attention. Empty praise is not fulfilling and won't mean anything to the young musician. Let the students have a feeling of worthiness for the compliment.

Wow! Fantastic! By George, you've got it! That's incredible! Dynamite! Spectacular! Cool, dude! Super work! Very creative! You're a real trouper! You learned it, all right! Outstanding! You just made my day! That's correct! Bravo! Great smile! Lookin' good! Way to rock and roll! Give yourselves a hand! Yahoo! YEA! WTG!

CHAPTER 7:
FROM THE LAND OF "BLAHS" TO THE LAND OF "AHS!"

RAZZLE-DAZZLE 'EM

What do Fred Astaire, Bob Fosse, the Radio City Rockettes, and Lady Gaga have in common? And before you answer, know that this celeb list is just the tip of the iceberg. Many other icons could be mentioned, but in the interest of time (and space), these are the celebrities I've chosen. The dancing phenomenons all have one thing that sets them apart: the amount of time spent on attention to detail.

Fred Astaire worked hours upon hours with his dance partners making sure every step was just right. Even in his private life, his attention to detail was obvious (matching the color of his socks and his sweaters or wearing a coordinating tie as a belt). Bob Fosse's attention to detail made him the unchallenged king of razzle-dazzle. Mr. Fosse worked in every facet of the theater and continually strove for perfection. The Rockettes are such a tight troupe of dancers; limb placement will make or break the choreography. Lady Gaga is involved in costuming, hairstyles, makeup, and choreography. She controls every detail of her performance because she wants everything to perfectly fit together.

Paying close attention to small details in the score will take you to the next level musically. Getting picky with your show will do the same thing. Many times the director is so close to the material and the performers that the obvious is overlooked. It helps to step back, grab a pen, and take notes. Or better yet, dust off the old camcorder and record the rehearsal.

While moving up the ladder and making overall improvements are the goals, be cautious not to throw out the baby with the bathwater. Sometimes a director can get so particular and fastidious with comments that students begin to turn off once the director starts giving notes. The "deer in the headlights look" spreads rapidly among students, and it is difficult to restore the positive energy.

Make Choices
Just decide on these show details; there's no right or wrong answer. Make a choice and insist your performers live with (or stand by) your decision.

Ladies—Earrings, fingernails (clear or colored), shoes, hair parts, hairstyles overall, body glitter spray, eyeglasses (for safety only), stage jewelry, color of hosiery, undergarments, piercings and tattoos, lip color, eye shadow colors, length of hems, posture, facial expressions, rehearsal etiquette.

Men—Tube or ankle socks, shoe color and style, pressed shirts, ironed pants, ties, jewelry, ball caps in rehearsal, rehearsal etiquette, eyeglasses (for safety only), tattoos and piercings, shirts buttoned or unbuttoned, sleeves rolled, stage makeup, tux jackets (buttoned or not), hairstyles, posture, facial expressions.

I'M JUST SAYING...

Former President Ronald Reagan learned early in life the importance of details and making decisions. As a young teen, he went to a shoemaker to have a pair of shoes custom-made. The shoemaker asked if he wanted a round toe or a square toe. The teenage Reagan couldn't make up his mind. A week later he went to pick up his shoes and he was in for a big surprise. One shoe had a round toe, while the other had a square toe. Reagan later said that pair of shoes taught him a life lesson: If you don't make your own decisions, somebody else will make them for you. Decide your show. Think about the details and step forward—hopefully with two matching shoes!

GREEN SKY

In my seventh year of teaching, I started to notice that many of my ensemble members would whisper comments each time I made a major announcement in rehearsal. I was concerned about the spreading secrecy and what I considered to be disrespectful behavior in the classroom. I couldn't quite make it out but it sounded as if the students were repeating the initials "G.S." I first tried  to ignore the situation, as the whispering would stop about as quickly as it started. Finally, my curiosity got the best of me. I called the two section leaders into my office.

I questioned the male and female section leaders about the meaning of the "G.S." nonsensical murmurings. The two seemed reluctant to explain the phrase and appeared rather embarrassed about being questioned. Finally, knowing I wasn't going to let them leave my office without cracking the code, the two ensemble members reluctantly explained that the initials G.S. stood for "Green Sky." Seeing that I still wasn't following, the male explained that each time I made a "this is what we are going to do" statement to the show choir, and the show choir thought the goal unattainable, the members would whisper among themselves, "Green Sky." Meaning if Mrs. Mack says the sky is green, then the sky is green.

Not totally following the logic and still fearing the worst, I asked them to continue explaining. The female said the singers basically had learned to trust me, the director. On a daily basis, I expected the members to do activities out of their box, to reach higher than any of them thought possible, and to basically achieve what they considered the impossible. They explained the group's apprehension in many performance areas including selection of literature, rehearsal schedules, costumes, costume changes, solo choices, personnel, performance venues, touring expectations, icebreaker games, the ridiculous amount of thank-you notes the singers were expected to write, the pyramid philosophy, and more. Basically the group had learned to accept and embrace my vision, no matter how unpopular my decisions.

That was a life-defining moment for me. I realized the great power and influence of a teacher, and that all of us need to use that power for good. The students were unquestioning in their loyalty and as an ensemble; they were confident that they wouldn't be embarrassed on stage or asked to do a task that I wouldn't do myself. **They trusted me completely.**

Wow! What a cool concept for teachers. And yet, with that simple phrase came even more responsibility. What a wonderful feeling to know my students respect my decisions each year, even if they don't totally understand or agree with what is being asked of them. It is important that the director does his or her homework, continues growing, and respects each member as he or she is given respect in return.

A second teaching highlight came about recently. A Latin/hip-hop musical, *In the Heights*, came on the scene, and I decided to introduce the awesome arrangement of the medley to the show choir. For the first time ever I began doubting myself. Rehearsal time was short, the style was new and challenging, our budget for costumes and a set was nonexistent, and the combo parts were wicked for the available rehearsal time. There was no way we could master all of this in just a few rehearsals. I told the students that I had made a mistake and that we would perform something less demanding and more attainable. The students rallied, saying, "Green Sky, Mrs. Mack." They believed they could get it done and had me believing as well. My students taught me to believe and to reach higher than I thought possible. And guess what? The medley turned out wonderfully and was a valuable teaching moment. What a "high" for all involved! ☺

OVER THE RAINBOW

Judy Garland sang it best. Hailing from the state of Kansas, I'll confess that I am a *Wizard of Oz* fan. In fact, if you want to program a popular piece of music, "Somewhere Over the Rainbow" was recently voted number one on the "Songs of the Century" list compiled by the Recording Industry Association of America and the National Endowment for the Arts. The American Film Institute also ranked "Over the Rainbow" the greatest movie song of all time. And yet, Judy Garland canceled many performances of this amazing piece because of vocal problems at the end of her career.

Teachers need to be reminded how fragile the vocal folds are and how easily they can be injured. God gave us one set of vocal cords. If we lose our ability to communicate, our schoolwork, home life, and personal life will suffer. At the end of Judy's career, she didn't sound the same as she did in her first "Rainbow" rendition. Years of vocal problems and vocal abuse were apparent. Hopefully we can learn from her vocal voyage.

Some years ago, I attended a voice-therapy workshop. A voice specialist shared his wisdom and I took notes like crazy during the two-hour session. At the end of the workshop, the "voice doctor" announced that his $1,000-an-hour fee was not nearly what he should be charging, as he worked with rock stars that were constantly battling with vocal health issues. I remember thinking, *Someday I'll write a book for music educators and I'll include a section on vocal health*. Readers, you're getting a $2,000 bonus with these included vocal tips. First-year teachers, this "Vocal Pedicure" is for you!

The following exercises should be repeated up to six times a day for serious vocal troubles:
- Roll head around very slowly two times each way with jaw hanging loosely.
- Yawn very lazily six times.
- Lie down and breathe low, chest calm, shoulders relaxed.
- Drop the jaw and pat lightly under chin for looseness. Wiggle jaw in a circular motion.
- Chew lazily and sloppily for one minute. Add sigh sliding downward with the voice. (Like a cow chewing its cud—don't do in public!)
- Massage sides of neck two times a day with thumb and middle finger.

Add the following sounds at each practice session:
- "My, oh, my, oh, my, oh" in a light sound, while rolling the neck, jaw, and head side to side.
- "Whom do you choose?" Each time the phrase is repeated, emphasize a different word—light, high voice.
- Falsetto singing for guys and a light, high voice for ladies. Encourage good breathing.
- Practice speaking in a Mickey Mouse voice or a Julia Child voice.
- Blurbles and rolling r's up and down the scale. These are good breath-connecters.

Points to be stressed:
- Watch the flow of words in conversation to avoid run-on sentences. Breathe often.
- Do not give vowels a glottal attack. Underline them in a song and rehearse correctly.
- Talk no more than absolutely necessary. Never yell to silence a class or shout over instruments.
- Use a soft-spoken voice and don't talk on your "cords." No yelling.
- Stay off the phone late at night when the voice is already exhausted.
- Use a microphone or amplified sound anytime possible.
- Maintain good posture. Only 20 percent of breath is utilized when using bad posture.

Vocal health tips:
- Limit caffeine, alcohol, tobacco, and red food coloring intake. They will all dry out the cords.
- Second-hand smoke also dries out the larynx.
- Use lots of inflection in the voice. Find your normal speaking range (don't talk on your "cords").
- Whispering should be avoided when the cords are tired.
- Drink eight to ten glasses of water a day.
- Keep mouth covered when jogging to avoid cold air hitting cords directly.
- Always use a good vocal warm-up before singing.

Promoting good vocal health:
- Avoid yelling and screaming—cheerleading is very bad on the vocal cords.
- Eliminate glottal attacks when singing and speaking.
- Do away with laughing uncontrollably and in an abusive manner.

- Be cautious about grunting when exercising and/or lifting weights.
- Stay away from noisy situations. Control background noise.
- Don't sing over the noise of the car radio and/or radio talking.
- Don't talk over others. It will strain your voice and add tension to an already fragile system.
- Use a humidifier in the winter to help alleviate dryness.
- Raise your hand to get the attention of a large group. Use a sound system.
- Don't yell or cheer at sporting events. Learn to clap hands and wave arms in support.
- Control the distance between you and a friend when speaking.
- **Best rule of thumb: If you can't reach out and touch them, don't try to talk to them.**

Conditions that will affect the voice:
- Allergy or upper respiratory infections will cause abuse to the voice. Stay away from antihistamines as they are drier-outers.
- The use of aspirin can increase the potential of hemorrhage of vocal fold blood vessels.
- During a female's menstrual period, the vocal cords will swell; avoid overuse of voice.
- Birth control pills can affect the top range for high sopranos.
- Coughing and excessive throat clearing will cause severe irritation and can actually cause more mucus to form. Try drinking water, swallowing, singing, or lightly coughing air through your throat.
- Airplane flights and long car rides tend to dry out the voice. Drink lots of water.
- Paint fumes and other chemicals can irritate the voice box.
- Heartburn and stomach acid are often hidden causes of voice irritation.

Voice therapy exercise:
- Quit talking. Use your face and hands to express the message.
- Think before you speak. Don't say it unless it is necessary communication.
- Text instead of speaking on the phone.
- Do not gargle; it forces unnecessary vibration on the vocal folds.
- Don't whisper; it put the folds in a state of tension that is potentially more damaging than yelling.
- Breathing steam at night can relax your vocal cords and lessen swelling.
- Neti pots are devises that can help irrigate nasal passages using salt water.
- Learn to listen.
- Consult your ENT (ears, nose and throat doctor) if conditions don't improve.

Maintain a practice of good vocal hygiene. Take good care of your instrument. It is the only one God gave you!

> **Take good care of your instrument.**

NO MARKING

When a person "marks" a combination, the individual is holding back and not performing full out. Instead of going for it, the performer is conserving energy and mentally rehearsing the routine or given exercise. Unfortunately, this quickly becomes habit and students forget to put it into high gear when they walk onto the stage.

Students need to rehearse in a lively manner and draw on performance-level energy from the beginning. Insist on good posture and energetic movements at all times. In other words, always rehearse the choreography, vocals, facials, and posture full out. The exception would be if a person was physically injured and needed to sit out or take a breather. In this case it would be best for the performer to mark the show than not participate at all.

Injuries can occur when students mark. A student may get into the spirit of things and add a double back tuck with a twist, knocking out his or her dance partner. OK, maybe that example was a bit extreme, but marking can throw off the choreography. Students can get hurt if spacing changes or if someone's arm or foot stretches farther than it did in rehearsal.

One of my vices in life? I admit to being a Diet Coke addict. I hate that my confession comes right after discussing vocal health and the importance of drinking water. I have rationalized my habit for a long time, but seeing it in print makes me realize I am not only a fanatic but am also rather particular about my indulgences. Certain fast food chains and specific restaurants have better soda mixes than others. Yes, I admit that I am a "Diet Coke snob" when it comes to mentioning the soft drink. What makes the Diet Coke different? The caffeine and the fizz! In my opinion, there are few things worse in life than a "flat" Diet Coke or a drink without caffeine. I mean, what's the point?

I've had days when my groups looked uncaffeinated and uncarbonated. Those were probably the days that my teaching was uncaffeinated and uncarbonated. Keep energy underneath, whether standing or sitting. Stretch the pose five more inches. If all of the background is involved, there won't be an energy roller coaster. After an intense rehearsal, students should barely have enough energy to walk out the door. Fatigue is contagious. Think yourself into an intense practice and don't think of it as a chore. Don't ever be like Morales in *A Chorus Line* and feel "Nothing."

- -

I'M JUST SAYING...

*I designed T-shirts for my tap classes at one time that read "Life is short. Don't mark!" And on the back, they read "**TAP LOUD!**" Maybe T-shirts that said "**SING LOUD**" wouldn't work out as well but perhaps "**LIVE LOUD!**" would have the same meaning. I also love the expression "Life is not a dress rehearsal." Live life to the fullest; we never know when it will be our last day.*

And my other favorite quotes about life:
"Think of all the women on the Titanic who skipped dessert."
"No day but today..."

—lyrics from Rent

- -

THE "B" WORD (BUDGET)

In the words of Kenny Rogers, "you've got to know when to hold 'em, know when to fold 'em." Poker may be an art form but it is also a game in which money is used to keep score. Whether we like the thought or not, budgets can sometimes make us feel as if we are playing a guessing game—gambling with money that may or may not be ours and then waiting to see how the cards are dealt.

Instead of sitting back and waiting for an ace that may never show, put together a plan for expenditures. Organize your financial plan and present it to your administrators, as if you were making a pitch for a presentation. Decide what is needed for the entire year. Compare sheet music to textbooks. Music is your textbook. Most courses use a textbook that may cost $50 to $100 depending on the subject.

When purchasing music, spend wisely. Decide if the arrangements could be reused. Avoid songs that are too repetitive—they are easy to teach, but choreography can become redundant. Have your singers, costumes, theme, and choreography in mind when selecting music. Teach students to share music with a folder partner to double the music library's literature.

While budgeting may be a game to some, it is becoming more of an important issue to teachers all the time. School systems are headed into new territory with the changes in the world's economy. Unemployment is on the rise. The arts, once essential in our schools and communities, are now being "viewed" as a frivolity instead of a necessity. We need to pull in our belts and prove that we can follow suit with the rest of the school system all the while presenting a first-rate program that involves a large percentage of participating students.

Alternative funding might be generated by putting on a talent show or a dessert concert. The proceeds from ticket sales could benefit the department or scholarship students needing costumes, or provide other needs in the department. Some universities charge a lab fee, an accompanist fee, or a music club fee. Athletic departments often charge rental fees for equipment and practice fields. Be sensitive to the students who are not able to "pay to play." Set up some type of a system for these students who want to be involved in music but lack funds. Many of these students are proud and do not want handouts. Work out a way to barter for students' talents: helping in the music library, building sets, cleaning rehearsal rooms, assisting with technology, or designing a Facebook page.

Document test scores, hours invested in the program (out of class time), retention efforts from involved students, and community impact. Present these numbers in a positive fashion at the next board meeting or PTA meeting. Decipher between wants and needs and don't get defensive. Remember, everyone else is fighting for their programs to survive as well.

I'M JUST SAYING...

Every deck of fifty-two cards has 2,598,960 possible hands. You will be dealt one of them. It is your choice what you do with that hand.

X = X

"X = X" is a meaningful and educational activity that I've used for years with all my musical ensembles. We complete the activity a week before each performance. When alums come in and visit a rehearsal, they can always tell if we've played the X = X game, as it makes that big of a difference in the performers and the performance. The X = X equation basically means that whatever emotions the students are feeling on stage, that is what the audience will be feeling. If the students are nervous, the audience will be nervous for them. If the students have no energy, the audience will be "dead" and nonresponsive. If the students are electric on stage, that will carry into the audience.

Students often interpret song lyrics differently. It is important to discuss the lyrics and figure out the single message the ensemble wishes to communicate. The piece may be layered with connotations (subtext) and the singers will discover nuances throughout the season. Work together as a team to uncover the text. As a result, during the performance, the audience will get a single emotion instead of mixed sentiments.

To play the X = X game, one person will jot down the suggestions that come from classmates. The director or a section leader will lead the discussion and take a few minutes for each song selection. To begin with, a volunteer will read the song lyrics as if reading a story. Students will then offer suggestions as to what emotion they feel best represents the entire song. Don't be surprised if the discussion turns passionate and heated as students take ownership in their performances and reveal how the piece speaks to them personally. Finally, vote on a single emotion for each selection in the show.

Emotions to consider for X = X include inner peace, love, contentment, joy, appreciation, passion, glee, astonishment, surprise, tenderness, yearning, sincerity, playfulness, hysteria, fear, pride, anger, envy, confidence, jealousy, vulnerability, apprehension, melancholy, flirtatiousness, embarrassment, determination, agitation, innocence, ambition, cockiness, courage, hope, trust, and gratitude. Of course the response must fit the libretto.

Try selecting different emotions, even if the songs in your set have similar lyrics and sentiments.

This trick will keep the show fresh for the performers and the audience. Write the show order on the poster and the elected emotion next to the song selection. Hang the poster in the rehearsal room so students will have a daily reminder of what they should be feeling and thinking as they sing the lyrics. Communicate with your audience through this thought process as well as the body and face. Great performers communicate with their audiences in a variety of ways.

I'M JUST SAYING...

In the future, if you are required to sit through a boring lecture or faculty meeting (I didn't say that!) and are struggling to stay alert and involved, try the X = X game. Change your thought process and get physically involved in the discussion. Start nodding your head (I refer to this trick as "doing the bobble head"), raise eyebrows, and change facial expressions. As you physically get involved and concentrate on an emotion, you will become interested and attentive. Try it sometime—it works!

YA GOTTA HAVE HEART AND MUSIC

Have you ever been a part of a rehearsal that seemed to drag on forever? Maybe the participants were barely staying awake in their seats, and the thought of having to actually stand up was almost intolerable. The minutes seemed to tick by and the hour was excruciating painful. And then, finally, the bell rang, signaling the end of the class. Everyone (including the director) exploded out of their seats, voices projecting loud and clear, tearing out of the room as fast as possible to go meet friends or to find food.

Everyone in the classroom was dead tired throughout the entire rehearsal and suddenly all this energy appears? What's the deal? It is a matter of deciding where to put your passion. If each person decided to apply that passion and energy to the rehearsal, the class would have had different results. The rehearsal atmosphere would be improved. This lesson applies to teachers and students alike.

The equation $2 + 2 = 4,000$ makes total sense if you've ever experienced the benefits of teamwork and synergy. If the director has an upbeat attitude, it will trickle down through the ranks. Find something to be passionate and excited about in each day. Dig deep. Instill proper mental attitude and enthusiasm so the room can bring to life the music and dance that is before them. Inspire from the beginning downbeat. Keep the rehearsals (and life) moving. If the literature you are rehearsing is exciting, most of your problems will be nonexistent. Motivate in a positive way.

Decide what your ensemble or department will stand for. If you don't stand for something, you'll fall for anything. Be passionate. An educator shouldn't be so concerned about only teaching students to sing and dance. Teach them life lessons and how to be better people through the vehicle of choir. The students will come back and say thanks many times over—for making them appreciate the arts and making them become better human beings.

My dad always told me that if I chose a career I loved, I'd never work a day in my life. It may sound cliché but it is true. Find new ways to love your job. Turn your job into a career. Maybe that means you go back to school to get more training. Or maybe it is time to make some changes. Instead of directing the church choir, join the hand bell choir or volunteer in the nursery. You'll have a new appreciation for the people around you. Stay fresh. Maybe you need to take a yoga class, change your diet, or stop hanging out in the teacher's lounge. Take a positive step today to improve your heart—and it will change your tune.

> My dad always told me that if I chose a career I loved, I'd never work a day in my life.

Whatever you choose to do in life, make sure it's something you're passionate about, because you'll be competing against people who are. Life is too short to be apathetic. Find a cause and go for it. Treasure every moment because the clock is running. Make the most of today and treasure it more because you shared it with people who share your zeal and heart for music. As the saying goes: *Yesterday is history. Tomorrow is a mystery. Today is a gift. That is why it is called the PRESENT!*

I'M JUST SAYING...

You've all seen choral groups that are so technically perfect, they create a level of perfection that seems untouchable. While these groups have artistry, the performance leaves the audience flat. If audience members want an experience devoid of emotion, they should stay home and listen to a professional recording. Mix heart and music in each and every rehearsal and it will be apparent in each performance.

CHAPTER 8:
BEHIND THE SCENES

BREAK A LEG

Athletic teams have been providing individuals with recognition and acknowledging team members' contributions for many years. Signs on lockers, posters with the team members' names, photo buttons of the players, team shirts, goody bags for long trips, announcing athletes' names at games, and pep rallies are ways the student body, community, and coaches encourage their players during the season. These signs and gifts of approval make a huge impact on the students and their self-worth.

It would be nice if everyone had someone in their corner to build them up. Many of our students today may not have family support, financial aid, and/or friends to give words of encouragement or root for them in the cheering section. The following ideas come from my book *Icebreakers 2: 64 More Games and Fun Activities* and will have a positive effect on the individual and his or her future attitude and success in your program. The results will be worth the time and trouble.

simple bravissimo! and "break-a-leg" ideas

47

IceBreakers 2: Retreat Makers – Building Relationships

Gathering these items may take some planning ahead, but students will be thrilled with your kind thoughts and actions. Many of your students will save the notes and little goodies for years. Corrections can help, but encouragement can even be a far greater help.

DIRECTIONS:

Type a note and place in a cellophane gift bag or a baggy (individually wrapped and still affordable for the director). Choose one or several of the following ideas. Parent groups could also help in collecting and distributing the "break-a-leg" notes and goodies.

- Atomic Fireball® - to light your fire when you feel burned out
- Band-Aid® - to remember to be kind and to not hurt each other
- Cinnamon candy – to stay "fired up" for the program
- Emery board – remember that when the going gets rough, you have friends you can turn to
- Eraser - to remind you that everyone makes mistakes, but friends (and music teachers) forgive
- Gum – for "chews"-ing to be in this musical ensemble and to remind you to stick with it
- Hershey® Hug and Kiss and Gummy Bears®- to remind you that you are loved.
- Laffy Taffy® - to remind you to take time to laugh
- Million Dollar® candy bar with a note "This is what you are really worth!"
- Musketeers® - to remind you that teamwork can be sweet!
- Payday® candy bar for accompanist, band members, and volunteers. "…Wish it could be more!"
- Penny - to always use good "cents"
- Peppermint – to remind you of your daily commit-"mint"
- Q-Tip® - to remind you to be a good listener
- Smarties® - Fine Arts students are the smartest around!
- Starburst® – to remind you to reach for the STARS
- Sunflower seeds or Planters® peanuts – to remind you to grow where you have been planted
- Teabag – because you are "tea"-rrific!
- Tea candle or birthday candle – to keep lighting the way for future students
- Tootsie Roll® – remember to be a "roll/role" model at all times
- Whoppers® - to remind you to always tell the truth

FAVORITE QUOTES TO SHARE WITH STUDENTS AND STAFF:
1. The woods would be silent if no birds sang, except the best!
2. Giving it another try is better than an alibi.
3. The smallest good deed is better than the grandest intention.
4. Looking at the bright side of things never hurt anyone's eyes.
5. Perfect practice makes perfect performance.
6. If you find a path without obstacles, chances are it doesn't lead anywhere!
7. To be happy, think happy!
8. Anytime's the right time for learning something new.
9. Success is a balance of hard work and talents.
10. Be a "fun-to-be-with" person but always make wise choices.
11. Believe in yourself. If you don't, no one else will either.
12. Practice and determination make a winning combination.
13. Problems are challenges in disguise.
14. A little extra effort turns "good" into "best!"
15. A smile is a gift you can give every day. ☺

BONUS QUOTES:

"We are what we repeatedly do; Excellence, then, is not an act, but a habit." ~ *Aristotle*

"To sing well and dance well is to be well-educated." ~ *Plato*

I C E B R E A K E R S

STAGE MANAGER

A stage manager provides organizational support to the director and the ensemble throughout the entire production. The stage manager is important to the whole process and will end up working side by side with the director. Finding the right personality is critical. This isn't a job for a power-hungry student, rather a job for the person with a servant-type attitude. A good stage manager also needs a working knowledge of the theater and music program.

Not every program is lucky enough to have the luxury of a stage manager. If a student has a passion for backstage work and an interest in this area, it can be a win-win situation for all involved. Always set ground rules for the stage manager and the performers to ensure a successful experience for all.

The stage manager can be assigned a variety of tasks such as marking dimensions on the floor, placing a number line or a center "X" (from which to determine stage spacing), and having props available for rehearsals. Other jobs might include recording light and sound cues, calling places before the curtains open, and keeping track of time during intermission. The director can then concentrate on what is most important—the musical portion and production of the show. Often on the day of a show, the stage manager must deal with technical and human crises that occur on the spot. Having the stage manager keep track of logistical and scheduling details is very helpful to the director.

The stage manager should have a health kit easily available backstage. The kit should include antiseptic, alcohol pads, a disposable instant cold pack, gauze pads, disposable vinyl (nonlatex) gloves, hard candy and packets of sugar (for diabetics), hydrocortisone cream, a lighter (to sterilize), moleskin, rubbing alcohol, saline, smelling salts, soap, a surgical mask, tampons, throat lozenges, tweezers, and water bottles.

A stage emergency kit should include batteries (extra), buttons (for tux jackets and tux shirts), crackers and peppermints (for upset stomachs), flashlights, safety pens, sewing kit (thread, needle, and mini scissors), medical release forms, and a large bottle of hand sanitizer.

I'M JUST SAYING...

My funniest stories are miscommunications that take place with stage managers. Over the years, I have been blessed with great stage managers; they've been patient, kind, and quick to pick up on the absurd backstage sign language that I've developed. For instance, the show choir recently performed outdoors at the Kansas State Fair. We were struggling with buzzing monitors so I put my index finger on my nose and flapped my elbow, while using my foot to motion to the monitor. The stage manager of course understood that meant "there is a buzz in the monitor"—as I was miming a bumblebee, which makes a buzzing sound. Unfortunately, the entire audience saw my ridiculous stage antics. The students got a good laugh watching the performance video.

Or the time I kept patting my heart and saying "top," which meant to start at the top of the show with the National Anthem. This time our signals were crossed and the stage manager thought that I had a problem with her top—or that it was too revealing. After several costume changes, she figured out that the show order was being changed and that was no wardrobe malfunction.

STRIKE!

Strike! For most students, saying goodbye is the hardest part of the performance. A performer is physically and mentally exhausted after the course of a performance or a season of show choir. The singers have invested time and energies, built sets, created props, worked on costumes, and felt a real sense of accomplishment and purpose. They worked together as a unit and a team. Now, the team members are asked to voluntarily turn around and tear the project apart with their bare hands. Everything they worked on is taken down, destroyed, or packed away. Makeup is wiped off for the last time and costumes are viewed to see who will wear them next.

The striking of a set is comparable to taking down the Christmas tree and putting away holiday decorations. When you decorate for the season, you don't think at all about the dreaded day when you must put away everything—the day that signifies the end of a magical time spent with family and friends, and the end of surprises, gifts, smiles, a few tears maybe, and great fellowship. But of course, it can't be Christmas all year long. One has to think about the New Year right around the corner and start looking ahead to the next stage of life. Believe it or not, transitions can be difficult for the directors and family members—not just for the students.

To ease the pain of saying farewell, I came up with few "strike" activities that seem to work. Remember, every ensemble has different challenges and needs. Create your own traditions.

> **Create your own traditions.**

Play uplifting "party" music throughout the strike process. The more upbeat the music's tempo, the faster the students will move. This will ensure a fun and light mood. Be sure everyone is involved. It will go faster and be more fun. Make a game of putting the stage or room back even better than when you started. Take photos when you finish.

A month or two before the last day of class (the dreaded day of handing in costumes and cleaning up), my ensemble does an early end-of-the-year activity. I have the materials ready and don't explain what we are doing or why. Each person gets a 4½- by 11-inch piece of paper with his or her name on top. I explain the rules: Once everyone is seated and has a colored marker, he or she is to pass the paper to the right. The papers will circle and students will write one positive word and sign their name under the encouraging word or memory on each page, one by one. I tell the students that I'll be collecting the papers so they must write only positive comments and G-rated memories.

Once the papers have circled completely around the room, I collect the papers—before any student gets to see the paper with his or her name on it. Then, I have the papers laminated and turn them into bookmarks. I hand them out at the end of the strike—during the final goodbye. Sometimes I also present students with a handwritten note, a DVD memory scrapbook, or a small token from the year. This farewell tradition helps ensure that the students do the strike in a timely fashion and that the job is done correctly. The students are excited to see what nice comments their friends wrote about them and what special memories were recorded on the bookmark.

I'M JUST SAYING...

> *At the end of the strike, invite ensemble members to make a time capsule about the show. Include photos of costumes and the set, goofy behind-the-scenes photos, a program, short memoirs from each performer, and even a DVD of the performance. After this tradition is established, students not will only make a time capsule for their year, but they can open up a capsule from the past.*

EMERGENCY KIT

Before loading the school vans or a bus for a performance, it seems that one performer or another regularly forgets or misplaces one part of the show choir costume, music, or something else extremely essential to the show's success. If you've ever traveled with students (or adults), I'm sure you can relate. This used to irritate me and ruin the bus ride, as I would worry and fret about how we were going to find a tux shop open at 8 a.m. on a Sunday, or where we would find a music store that carried drumsticks and brushes. (True story, I had a drummer who on one major occasion forgot his drumsticks!) Of course the forgetfulness was never realized until the bus was well on its way—miles from any type of civilization.

I have learned a few tricks over the years. Instead of totally stressing out about the situation, always bring along an emergency travel kit. This doesn't mean that students get to be irresponsible; each time an item is forgotten, the cost will be deducted from the student's personal show choir account. It seems students are much more reliable when their own money is involved. Students who complain have a choice. They can choose not to perform (which may affect their ensemble grade) or they can work off the infraction by washing uniforms, ironing pants, sewing on buttons, replacing sequins, and so on.

SHOW CHOIR EMERGENCY TRAVEL KIT:

- antistatic spray
- black duct tape
- bobby pins
- candy (for diabetic students)
- contact solution
- cough drops
- drumsticks (seriously)
- earring backs (eight extra)
- earrings (four extra pairs)
- fingernail polish remover
- folder of music (for instrumentalists)
- hairspray
- ladies tights (four extra pairs)
- makeup (eye color, blush, lipstick, eyeliner, mascara)
- men's black tube socks (four extra pairs)
- nail polish (for runs in hosiery)
- needle and thread
- safety pins
- spankies (bloomers)
- spray deodorant
- tampons
- Tide stick (to spot clean small stains)
- ties (for each color of shirt—two extra)
- tissues
- travel-size hair spray
- water bottles

I'M JUST SAYING...

And the most important item in the emergency kit? Black duct tape. The tape can be used to clamp risers, hem pants, tape ankles (replacing black socks), reduce slick spots on shoes, remove lint from costumes, stick on earring backs, mark the stage, and tape microphone switches to an "on" position. One time a student forgot his black bow tie and created a "duct tape tie." Remember Bart from page 89? He's that guy who saved the day by designing a bow tie from duct tape.

TOP TWENTY-TWO TRICKS OF THE TRADE

Every show choir has their own tricks. These are a few that I've either heard through the grapevine or that I've used myself because of costume malfunctions, slippery risers, faulty props, dark stages, glitches in scenery, or for whatever reason. More tricks are being developed on a daily basis, as show choir is ever-evolving.

1) **Breaking in new dance shoes:** Wear the dance shoes around the house with two pairs of thick socks. Take the shoes in your hand and bend the toe back and forth.

2) **Dance shoes are too slick:** Use masking tape on the bottom of the shoe; rub sand paper on the bottom of the shoe; pour cola on the sidewalk and walk through it several times. Don't use diet cola—the sugar is what keeps the shoes from sliding. Or, do the Twist out on the street. The asphalt will rough up the bottoms of the shoes.

3) **Keeping shoes shined:** Use a regular shoeshine kit; shine shoes with Avon's Skin So Soft; shine shoes with a light coat of petroleum jelly; or use pretreated shoeshine cloths.

4) **Shirttails that keep falling out:** Tuck shirttails into underwear, pulling the bottom tabs of the shirt through the underwear legs to the front, or use safety pins on the shirts if the performers don't have any fast costume changes. Girls wearing shirts can tuck them into their spankies.

5) **Drooping dress straps:** Use Firm Grip spray-on glue on shoulders, or use toupee tape.

6) **Sequins that cut under the arms of the ladies' dresses:** Spray hairspray on the edges or apply the tape used to fasten wrestling mats together. Clear tape will also work.

7) **Clingy or staticky garments:** Place a few drops of water under the dress, put hairspray on the men's socks or nylons, or use antistatic spray. Rub hand cream over men's socks or nylons, or on top of a slip. Using WD-40 on the body also lessens cling.

8) **Fragrances on the stage:** Many students have allergies. Use unscented deodorants and no perfume.

9) **Emergency tap shoes:** Duct-tape spoons on the bottom of shoes, or have your drummer create tap sounds while a dancer mimes the tap steps.

10) **Needing more body definition:** Bronzer can give the illusion of muscles for guys and cleavage for ladies.

11) **Puffy eyes:** Put two spoons in the freezer for ten minutes. Place the spoons under eyes to get rid of swollen eyes. Use highlighting shadow to brighten your eyes and lift the look of your whole face.

12) **Makeup not staying:** Close your eyes and spray hairspray over your face to set makeup.

13) **Lips sticking to teeth:** Use petroleum jelly on lips and teeth to unstick lips and make teeth shiny.

14) **Acne and spots appearing on face:** Use toothpaste on skin to help tone down the redness.

15) **Hair problems:** Don't wash hair daily. Hair extensions will give volume and length, or use wigs.

16) **Skin appearing washed out with certain costumes:** Be safe and use bronzer or spray tan rather than spending time in the sun. Choose colors that look good on all skin tones.

17) **Outfits falling off hangers and being misplaced:** Every student needs a garment bag with his or her name written on the front. Ladies should buy longer bags for their longer-length dresses. Use clothespins to keep outfits on hangers, or fold items over the hanger.

18) **Feeling weak and ready to pass out on stage:** Keep knees bent. If going down, sit instead of taking out an entire row of people. Have a signal in your choir and squeeze the hand of a person next to you if you feel faint. Encourage choir members to drink lots of water before performances.

19) **Whiten teeth:** Mix unused kitty liter and toothpaste. (Honest-to-goodness trick.) However, kids, I wouldn't try this at home!

20) **Feeling sick or nauseous:** Many times these are signs that students are dehydrated. Encourage drinking more water than normal. Between stage lights, costume layers, fast food, and hectic schedules, the factors add up. Keep crackers on hand.

21) **Forgotten black socks:** Duct-tape the ankles with black tape, and quickly rip it off after the show. The guy will never again forget his black socks! Forgotten black shoes? Use black socks.

22) **Face tips:** A lip brush gives you the most precision in applying lipstick. Set face one more time with powder to ensure a longer-lasting look. Date all makeup when you buy it. Replace mascara after three months to avoid clumping and bacteria. But save your old brush: Cleaned with eye-makeup remover, it's a handy declumping tool.

PUBLIC RELATIONS

This is one of my favorite stories and I try to frequently remind myself of the happy outcome, compared to what could have been. Thankfully, God looks after us and sometimes sends friends to be the voice of good and reason.

We were in the middle of show choir camp a few summers ago. Midweek is a hectic time for the staff, and about midnight we were having a staff meeting for the camp counselors and staff in the dorm lobby. We had reserved the room and about twenty-five of us had gathered. The counselors had been given several boxes of pizza and cans of soda but were frankly too tired to munch. Several football players were on campus for summer football training, and the guys were in the next room making quite a racket. I went in and politely but firmly asked them to be quiet as we had an important camp meeting taking place in the next room.

I am used to being treated with respect when asking students to abide by school rules and thought I had made myself clear. But not even five minutes later, the football players were once again disturbing "our" peace. Angrily I jumped up and hollered that I was calling security and then would be calling the football coach. I knew the players would have to run laps and would never misbehave again, maybe for the rest of their lives—if they lived past the next practice. I knew the coaches would take care of any disrespectful behavior.

Before I could make the call, I noticed our camp "mom," Nancy, calmly gathering up the pizza boxes and extra cans of soda. She made her way into the next room. Suddenly we heard applause and then silence. We continued with our meeting. I later asked Nancy what she had said to the athletes. She said she had taken them the leftover pizza and soda, told the football players to enjoy the goodies from our camp staff, and invited them to the final concert—with comp tickets, of course.

Not only did the players open doors for our campers the rest of camp, but the whole team showed up at the concert and made an enthusiastic, supportive audience. In fact, for as long as those guys were on campus, many of the team members showed up at various fine arts events—not because they were forced to, but because of the great PR and foundation of friendship laid early on by someone's creative thinking and caring spirit.

Why can't we all think out of the box and do what is kind and caring? Instead of ruining the relations between departments, we (thanks to Nancy!) made a positive impact with long-lasting results. The next time you have a problem to solve, decide if there are other kinder ways to fix it and what benefits can result.

The best PR for the department comes from within. Students and alums will be your best PR, for they have a natural inclination to be a part of success. Fliers, TV spots, and radio announcements have little effect these days, as we are flooded with media ads and information. Word of mouth and anecdotal stories are effective PR tactics. Start early by visiting grade schools and middle schools with your singers. Respect, reflect, and represent at all times. Old-fashioned manners never go out of style. When people are treated with respect, everyone benefits.

COLLABORATION

What are ways to work with other departments at your school? It is important to think of cocurricular and interdepartmental activities and collaboration. My college, Butler, has a history of nationally ranked football teams. To honor the football program, our show choir did a "football hero" medley ending with a national championship photo of the entire team—including all the coaches. This was a big hit in the community and pleased the coaches at the same time. It is ridiculous not to get along with the other departments in your school. At Butler, we share the same gym space for our show choir camp, and athletes and musicians may be in the same classes. We need to get along for recruiting and retention. When one department shines, it reflects on all the other departments.

> It is important to strive to be the best we can be while at the same time making those around us look good.

When selecting material, assess the musical *and* dance talents of your students. Don't select a *42nd Street* medley if you don't have a tap teacher nearby or the accessibility of tap shoes. Definitely think twice about producing *Seven Brides for Seven Brothers* if only six guys show up to audition. Identify your students' strengths and weaknesses. Showcase your students' versatility and let them shine! Be relentless in your search for the right material for your program. All good works of art have unity as well as variety.

Share your vision with the entire creative team. It can be frustrating for everyone involved in last-minute changes, undesirable cuts, or an ill-defined concept. Be sure that the pit orchestra can perform the desired tempos and that its members have been given all of the rehearsal information. Lack of communication creates stress and duress during musical rehearsals. Insist upon written notes from the choreographer that include dance notes and formations. This will help the director and the students, and will assure that the choreographer is prepared. The choreography presented first will be remembered when performance time comes. Don't allow staging changes unless a crisis ensues. Above all, stick to the rehearsal schedule. If you're in the middle of *The Music Man* and "Shi-Poo-Pi" is supposed to be taught the second week of rehearsal, be sure it gets taught!

Many times we make things more complicated than necessary. Remember these simple rudimentary ideas that make the teaching and learning manageable. Ask the theater department for help with sets and lights. Offer to share your number line, costumes, mirrors, etc. Work with the band director and perform a vocal and instrumental number as a finale. It will be a win-win situation for all involved. Attend and applaud achievements of other programs.

When all else fails ... hire a choreographer! Provide a recording and written music with marks. Tell the choreographer about your ensemble, outfits, age, experience, and strengths, and discuss fees beforehand. Share your vision for the piece, including concept and the function in the show. Be sure your students are present and ready (with dance shoes and nametags). The director must be present so he or she knows the style once the choreographer leaves. Don't sign up the ballet teacher in town or the PE instructor unless he or she has an understanding of vocal production. Check around to find professionals who comprehend the union of music and dance. Dream big. If you can imagine it, it can be achieved with the right choreographic tools and the right people.

Show choir competitions offer innovative ideas as directors collaborate with other directors. Show choir adjudication festivals can offer an environment where students and directors can learn professional entertainment techniques, share information, and showcase themselves to an interested and appreciative audience, finding respect among their peers.

CHAPTER 9:
TAKE A BOW

APPLAUSE

"What is it that we're living for? Applause, applause!" are the key lyrics from the award-winning Broadway musical *Applause* by Lee Adams and Charles Strouse. If this is truly what you are living for, you are going to have one sorry and unfulfilled ride. If your students agree, and if applause is the only thing in their lives that "brings on the glow," they too are going to have an empty feeling at the end of the voyage.

Early in my career, I invited John Jacobson and Mac Huff to present a show choir workshop for high school and college musicians in our area. During a question-and-answer period, a student asked Mac if he loved hearing audiences cheer for his arrangements and compositions. I'll never forget Mac's answer. He cautioned the students, saying that if they were in the music performance business for the sound of applause, they would be happy about 1/100th of the time. He said that they would spend most of their time in rehearsal and that if they didn't love to rehearse, they should find something else to do with their lives.

It is about the journey and not the final destination. Many times educators get so excited about reaching goals that we forget to enjoy the view along the way. How many times have we finished a concert and realized that the best

> Enjoy the "a-ha!" moments that happen along the way. The times that students really "get it" is the motivation for many of us to continue in the teaching profession.

moments of the rehearsal process took place sometime other than the night of the performance? Enjoy the "a-ha!" moments that happen along the way.

Applause can be a positive thing as we remember to applaud the efforts of others. Don't forget to show gratitude to the colleagues, parents, students, and administrators who helped make the performance a success. Triple-check the acknowledgments listed in the program so that no important names are omitted. Sometimes it is better not to list names in the program so that you don't inadvertently leave out any names.

Other ways to show the group's appreciation would be to sing a song to—or dedicate it to—the special people. The first song my singers learn on day one is a song from the musical *Scrooge* called "Thank You Very Much." It is amazing how many times we sing that number throughout the season. The students love to see the joy on the people receiving the message in song. Small gifts, plants, cards, posters, postcards, and singing telegrams are additional ways to show thanks and recognize individual's contributions.

Sometimes students may not appreciate the teacher's efforts until a later time—after the students have matured. It might take years of reflection, but more often than not, students will come back to say what a difference the music made in their life.

I'M JUST SAYING...

It is exciting when applause comes full circle. I remember applauding a student's efforts for auditioning after he had taken several years off from school and his life was at a standstill. Fast-forward a year and then seeing that student applauded as a professional performer at Disney World. The "Thanks, Mrs. Mack" and the accompanying wink from Prince Charming made me realize exactly why I became a teacher. Appreciate what you have been given and be thankful that you can live your dreams every day.

TODAY'S SHOW CHOIR SHOWDOWN!

In Fall 2010, *The TODAY Show* with Kathie Lee and Hoda sponsored a contest for show choirs. The winning group would receive an all-expenses-paid trip to New York City including a performance on *TODAY* and tickets to see a Broadway show. At first, I considered it just one of several show choir contests and competitions of late. Frankly this was something I knew my show choir, the Butler Headliners, didn't have the time, resources, and/or finances to get involved in, as we had a busy fall semester planned. After receiving hundreds of Facebook messages, texts, e-mails, and phone messages from alums around the country, all saying, "This is something the Headliners should enter," I decided that perhaps it was a sign and that I should reconsider. I read the official rules (important first step) and my section leaders offered to write the three-hundred-word entry essay. We were ready for the next step.

The second requirement was to record a three-minute DVD of a Headliner performance. I chose a song called "Heart and Music" and decided to pair it with the up-tempo number "Higher Ground." I felt those pieces described the Headliners while showing versatility in their musical and dance styles. Next, we had to find the time to make the recording. I was determined that we would not sacrifice class time and that the students wouldn't miss any class for the taping. Three days before entry deadline, the Headliners recorded the performance. I decided to take one for the team and miss an hour of the teacher in-service. One of my students owned a hand-held portable camera and after three takes, he was out of battery and we were out of time. The recording would have to do.

The next day, using the contest instructions, we tried to send the video file to the NBC studios, but we weren't able to get through. We finally called and found out that so many schools were sending videos that a server had gone down. That shouldn't surprise any of you out there reading this. Music teachers are known for their right-brain creative thinking. Meeting deadlines isn't normally an artist's cup of tea.

Another good omen: In August, the Butler president and vice president approved a new full-time vocal music position for the Butler Vocal Music Department. In a time of budget cuts, the additional position was an unexpected and incredible gift to the department. Instead of questioning, we rejoiced and hired a talented, young professional by the name of Matthew Udland. Mr. Udland has many gifts (master pumpkin carver) but also possesses an amazing ability to do almost anything tech-related. Somehow, Matt kept his wits about him and continued through the night to ensure that our video made it into the hands of The *TODAY* Show producers before the contest cutoff.

From the entry to selection it was a whirlwind. We received a call from a *TODAY* producer late on a Tuesday afternoon but were told we could not share the news about being a finalist until *TODAY* hosts officially announced it on the show. The electronic ballot voting started the next day. By 6:00 a.m. on Friday, two huge trucks and a semi were parked in the Butler parking lot with satellite dishes ready to record live in front of millions of viewers. All of this transpired in less than two and a half days.

The NBC producers said one reason the Butler Headliners were selected among the four finalists was the entry essay. They felt that it demonstrated lots of heart and that the ensemble had talent and much to offer to the 8.5 million people in their television viewing audience.

This is the essay that the Headliners sent to *The TODAY Show*.

The *TODAY* Show Choir Showdown
Butler Headliners
Director, Valerie Lippoldt Mack

The Butler Community College Headliners from El Dorado, Kansas believe there can be no music without heart and no song without passion. Striving to better the lives of others by reaching a "higher ground" through song and dance, the Headliners feel privileged to represent Butler as well as sharing their love for show choir each time the group takes the stage.

Under the direction of Valerie Lippoldt Mack, the Headliners consider themselves a close-knit family. Mrs. Mack challenges her students to be better performers while teaching life lessons. Butler alums can be found on Broadway, performing at Disney World, working at Carnegie Hall, teaching music, running dance studios, directing professional barbershop quartets, and as patrons of the arts. Still others can be found on cruise ships, as Miss America contestants, and as TV personalities. All will agree that the number one thing they learned through the Butler show choir experience wasn't the performance skills, but the education in life.

Headliner style is a fusion of hip-hop, music theatre and original heartwarming ballads. Over twenty compositions have been written and arranged specifically for the Butler Headliners' unique flavor.

Each show is filled with anticipatory electricity. Audiences across the nation have been delighted and continue to talk about their Headliner experience. Crowds are ignited with a message of hope and joy, making every Headliner performance memorable.

The Headliner members come from small Kansas farming communities, inner cities and military bases. Several have parents overseas who have yet to see a Headliner performance. It would be an honor and a dream come true to have the opportunity to share our heart and music with the world. Ya gotta have "HEART AND MUSIC!"

-The Butler Headliners

To prepare for the live question-and-answer session with Kathie Lee and Hoda was impossible. The group was not given any clue as to what might be asked or said.

If you or your students ever work in live television, here are some rules of thumb that will prepare them for any situation.

1) Be prepared for a hurry-up-and-wait game.

2) Reserve energy. You may be in front of the cameras for a long time before actually being seen and/or answering questions.

3) Take a moment and carefully listen to what is being said. Don't talk for the sake of talking.

4) When looking at the camera, think about the individual behind the camera. Visualize that you are speaking to one person at a time.

5) Do your homework. Reread the essay (or other submitted materials) and know what was previously said.

6) Answer honestly without trying to give the answers that you think they might want to hear.

7) Be specific in the answers. Don't be vague, but answer with precise examples.

8) Watch the clock and keep aware of time, as you may get cut off in the middle of a sentence.

9) Project a vibrant and winning attitude and spirit. Project confidence at all times.

10) Stand tall, or sit as if standing. Keep eyebrows slightly raised. Pull shoulders back and think about posture.

11) Prepare to react in a kind and professional manner no matter the outcome. Remember, you are already a winner for stepping out and taking a chance.

12) Answer from your heart.

13) Maintain composure and keep all answers in a positive nature.

14) Trust and believe in yourself. The answers are already there. Now be excited to share your vision and passion with others.

15) Dress professionally—as if auditioning. When you feel good about yourself, you will exude confidence and assurance in the answers.

16) Enjoy the moment. You may never have this opportunity again. Know that you are helping create memories that will last a lifetime—even though it will be just a few seconds of air time.

17) Stay focused and don't let comments, movement, or commotion break your focused concentration.

18) Don't be afraid to smile and have fun. Show your personality. We don't want to hear someone else's words coming out of you.

19) The only constant in life and live TV is change. Be flexible and learn to go with the flow. It can be even more impressive when the person(s) interviewed can think quickly and pick up the pieces.

20) Be sure to thank everyone involved—on camera and off.

When all was said and done, the Headliners didn't come in first but were told it was a close race. A special moment at contest's end was seeing the Butler students react after the announcement of the winning choir. The Butler Headliners stood up and gave the first-place show choir from Orlando, Florida, a rousing ovation. They then went to their Facebook and e-mail accounts to congratulate all the schools involved and to thank the *TODAY* staff. At that point, I knew that I had done my job.

The Butler Headliners did what they were supposed to do and they handled the stress and the whirlwind of activity with dignity. The community, alums, and friends and family members of the Headliners made us feel like winners. It was an amazing two days and was life-changing for many of the students. It brought great national attention to show choirs everywhere.

I told the Headliners when we first sent in the entry that it was a one in a million shot to be selected as a finalist. However, I told them, if we didn't give it a shot, it would be zero in a million. A few weeks later, I heard my words being quoted when one of the members decided to audition for a big show. I know the lessons learned will long stick with members of the group that had the experience *The TODAY Show* gave them.

Looking back, I'm glad we decided to take a chance and step out from our comfort zone.

> **It was a one in a million shot to be selected as a finalist. But if we hadn't given it a shot at all, our chances would have been zero in a million.**

FINALE
Whether it's the final chapter … or your final number … or the final show of the year, part of your brain is saying, *OK, we did it, now let's celebrate.* And then there's the part of the brain that won't shut off and is saying, *Hmmm … that song I heard on the radio on the way here tonight just might make a great closing number. And the dress on the woman standing in line at the drinking fountain—the coral shade might just be perfect for the girls' group next year.* Creative juices start flowing and somehow, no matter how exhausted you are, that little idea in your gut begins to materialize and suddenly you are ready to start up again. Somehow, energy surges out of your body and you once again are ready to tackle a new show, new group, or a new school, whatever the case may be.

Before jumping in with both feet, take some time for yourself and let your musicians bask in the glory of the final performance. Be careful, as burnout can occur for the director, the performers, and even the audience. Take a big breath and find some time for yourself. The students need a breather and you need to spend time by yourself to refuel and replenish. Your loved ones also need some of your time. Enjoy spending time with family and friends before jumping right back in.

After every show we do a "braggin' right circle." Each person shares a "brag" about the show and the person on his or her right. After one student finishes, the person to the **right** brags about the person on his or her right and so on—thus the "braggin' **right** circle." Students can mention the nice things they witnessed backstage, offstage, onstage, before the show, or cleaning up; the hard work; the growth of the students and the group; or whatever is on their minds. This is a chance to pay it forward.

Reflection is one of the best opportunities for the director and all the performers to grow and learn. Take time to reflect on the performance and all that went into making it the best it could be. Could things could be improved upon for the next show? Make a list and document the ideas. The performers and group will better themselves each time this happens. Don't take Dory's advice from the Disney movie *Finding Nemo* and "just keep swimmin'." The director needs to have a plan for improvement. Move forward on purpose—avoid treading water or dog paddling, merely attempting to stay afloat. "Let us run with endurance the race that is set before us" is a favorite passage of mine.

Right at this moment, we each have different reasons to smile. You can be passionate about something and still enjoy the journey. Don't take yourself or this thing called "show choir" or "music education" too seriously. Remember, life is not a dress rehearsal. Reflect, refresh, revisit, renew—and then it is time to start rebuilding once again.

Remember Dorothy's final words in *The Wizard of Oz*: "Toto, we're home! Home! And I'm not gonna leave here ever, ever again because I love you all! And oh, Auntie Em, there's no place like home." Enjoy the ride, but don't forget to come back home to rest and reboot the engine.

THE REVIEWS ARE IN

The reviews are in. Take time to listen to critics, not just to close friends who will give only positive assessments and tell us exactly what we want to hear. It's as if we tried on the dreaded swimsuit and then asked friends how we look. Friends will be kind, but their final analysis may not be what we need to hear.

If the appraisal is painful, we need to be honest with ourselves, as normally there is some truth in most of the critiques we read and/or hear about our performances. Because of intense involvement, expenditure of time, effort, and energy, and throwing ourselves into the mix, we are often too close to the project to see clearly.

When I was a child, our family would often take long car trips, and I vividly remember driving through miles and miles of farmland, watching wheat fields and cornfields whiz by. Row after row of wheat shocks mostly made me dizzy and I would be ready for a change in pace and eager for a different landscape.

Then came the day we took our first airplane ride. The view was completely different now, and as we soared, I couldn't believe how the farmland made such beautiful patchwork quilts. The woven pattern of colors was breathtaking from the aerial viewpoint.
Sometimes when working in the same old routine, we can't imagine the finished product. What seems redundant and meaningless in class is far from pointless in the greater scheme of things. Teachers and students have to hang on long enough to get a view of the seeds that have been sown from above.

Keep moving forward, even if those around you seem to be running out of steam or, worse yet, running on empty. Sometimes the journey will be steady and balanced. Other times you may be fighting an uphill battle or descending in a downward spiral. Enjoy each step of the journey and figure out a way to grow yourself and your students. Teach life lessons along the way. Your students will be only as good as what you demand of them. Your students don't care how much you know until they know how much you care. Believe in your students. If you love and respect them, they will love and respect you, the instructor.

I'M JUST SAYING...

At our annual beginning-of-the-year retreat, I ask the students to each name three people who helped them get to where they are right now, on a scholarship in our college's music department. Names are recited around the glowing campfire, and the following class period, I provide paper and envelopes so the students can personally write and thank those three people. The music students often mention parents, grandparents, family members, friends, and former members of the college music program. Usually, the students will also mention a teacher ... but not just any teacher. Without a doubt, the students will talk about their music teachers and how thankful they are for the love and encouragement they received. It is about then that each student gets emotional and passes to the next person in the circle. Teachers, you may not realize it, but you are making a huge difference in the lives of many. Thanks for the impact you are making. May you continue to find the strength, energy and resources to carry on.

SRO (STANDING ROOM ONLY)

Here are some of the lessons I've learned along the way, in and out of the classroom. Some of these are new bits of advice while some are suggestions from other chapters that bear repeating. I'm also throwing in quotes I've heard friends use and a few clichés. So, here they all are—in no particular order. Take a big breath, then read on for some ideas to improve your show so you can achieve a standing room only crowd—every show!

> **You can achieve a standing room only crowd—every show!**

HOW TO ACHIEVE STANDING ROOM ONLY (SRO)

- Make your choir something students can't live without.
- Be passionate about what you're doing. If the fire flickers, do something else.
- Let someone else step in who is ready to blaze a new trail.
- Quit complaining about the past. Good teachers change with the times.
- Keep growing. Don't ever sit or stand still. You will get there if you keep taking one step at a time.
- Perfection is never attainable, but keep striving. This is the concept of Kaizen (the road to perfection).
- Teach respect.
- Expect more than possible. Accept nothing less.
- Don't expect your students to do things that you wouldn't do yourself. Work together.
- Teach the "silver box" concept of using kind words and showing appreciation. It's as if you give a gift to others with your encouraging words.
- Expect and demonstrate professionalism.
- No lukewarm "stuff" in life or onstage. Be hot or cold. Make decisions and don't falter.
- Never teach from the piano or from one single area in the room. Move around.
- Don't sing along with your students. It will hurt them (and your voice) in the long run.
- Treat guests and audiences with the utmost respect.
- Fatigue is contagious.
- If someone's cell phone goes off in class or if someone texts … he or she brings TREATS for the class! (Cell phone interruptions are a pet peeve of mine, can you tell?)
- Bring in experts to critique and be involved in your program. Handpick loyal friends.
- No offensive jokes. If a remark or joke offends one person, it can't be performed on stage.
- Don't demand concentration unless you provide the environment.
- Be a part of your school and community. You are not a one-man show.
- Be trained in music and dance. Use correct terminology.
- Enjoy the journey. The process is more important than the product.
- Balance your life and your career!
- Celebrate your students' differences and uniqueness; don't judge.

- Wake up with an opportunity clock instead of an alarm clock. (Paul Gulsvig)
- Don't do anything that isn't fun! (No more Indian food, horror flicks, or treadmills for me!)
- If you're dancing the right choreography in the wrong window, it is the wrong choreography.
- Good leaders lead when no one is looking.
- Be prepared for the unexpected. A good disciplinarian anticipates problems before they occur.
- You have all the crayons—now color the picture. (Stephen Todd)
- God gave you two eyes, two ears, and one mouth. Those who are successful know how to use them in the correct proportion.
- When working transitions and applause, start the next piece at the height of the applause. It will keep the show exciting and moving.
- Never embarrass your students with embarrassing material.
- Be well-rounded. Embrace every situation and learn from it all. You can't put a price tag on education.
- Lighten up a bit. Remember … it's only show choir! What will the dash between the dates on your tombstone represent? Be a student of life!
- Master technique, then forget about it and perform.
- If you're teaching a sixty-minute class, plan for a ninety-minute class.
- Appearance is important: An audience first "hears" what you look like.
- The hardest part of being a good teacher is that you have to do it every day.
- Rehearse at performance level. Excellence is not an act but a habit.

PROGRAM NOTES (BONUS!)

ENCORE

You have been such a great audience that you've earned an encore! Wikipedia describes an encore as an additional performance added to the end of a concert. The word means "some more." Multiple encores are not uncommon. Encores originated spontaneously, when audiences would continue to applaud and demand more performance from an artist after the concert ended. In some modern circumstances, encores have come to be expected, and artists often plan their encores. Traditionally, in a concert that has a printed set list for the audience, encores are not listed, whether they are planned or spontaneous.

In the early days of modern rock music, Elvis Presley never played encores—a practice his manager felt was the best teaser to leave audiences wanting more. The now-famous phrase "Elvis has left the building" was used at the beginning of his career when Presley was not the headliner, followed by a plea for the audience to return to their seats to watch the rest of the show. Once he became a headliner, it was invariably followed by a polite "Thank you, and good night," to indicate to those present at the concert that there was not going to be an encore.

So, here is "a little more." The best tidbits were saved for the end. Enjoy ... and "THANK YOU VERY MUCH!"

1) **Respect can make or break your program.** Respect colleagues, students, parents, administration, and members in the community.

2) **Surround yourself with positive.** If you don't, you will drain precious time and energy from being your best.

3) Disorganization can close doors. If you can't organize, find someone who can help.

4) Faculty and student guidelines: Always arrive early, dress professionally, make class and rehearsals a priority, make smart decisions in and out of class, be honest and dependable, communicate, be a team member, practice good grooming, and **keep a positive attitude**.

5) If a student suddenly doesn't feel comfortable with singing certain lyrics or dancing, don't make a big deal of it, but be sure to address the situation privately. Other students shouldn't feel guilty. Don't reward or embarrass the student.

6) Help feeder programs. Take groups out to perform, offer shadow days, and send notes and e-mails of encouragement.

7) Memorization. **Don't give the option of not memorizing.** Memorize in sections, with physical actions; keep eyes closed; emphasize keywords; learn choreography in sections and work on the bow choreography early. For both singing and dancing, break it down, and learn the last section first.

8) Say 10 percent of what you are thinking—write even less. (Think Facebook!)

9) Promptness. Make it painful to miss or be late to a rehearsal. Better yet, **make rehearsals where students want to be.**

10) **Don't talk the talk but walk the walk.** "Teach—but only when necessary, use words". ~ Pastor Tom Harmon, Risen Savior Lutheran Church, Wichita, Kansas

11) Support all programs and departments in your school. You are not an island.

12) **Drink lots of water. Stay healthy.** If you are not the best you can be, you can't take care of your family or your students!

13) Don't start bad habits, and if you have any, get rid of them before you start rehearsing. Your choices don't affect just you but will domino across the board, like ripples in the water.

14) **Appreciate the life lessons you receive.** Journal the lessons so you can look back on them someday.

15) "You get out of life (and school) what you put into it." ~ Casey Durbin, Butler alum and a face (not a fur) at Walt Disney World.

16) **Faith—believe in yourself.** You have to believe in yourself if you want others to believe in you.

17) Take care of the important, not the urgent.

18) Instead of saying "5-6-7-8" to start the piece, save time with "7-8."

19) Exciting rehearsal = exciting product. It is the process we should be concerned about.

20) Leaders have vision and see beyond what everyone else sees.

21) "**A pair of shoes can change your life.** Just ask Cinderella." ~ Anonymous

22) "To sing well and to dance well is to be well-educated." ~ Plato (c. 428-348 B.C.)

23) Every once in a while—plant your feet and sing. Don't pace or add movement without a reason.

24) Life isn't about how to survive the storm, but **how to dance in the rain**.

25) Learning is not a spectator sport.

26) Acknowledge what your singers are doing right and let them know—and let them know often.

27) Put the most effort into the song you like the least.

28) WHAT (you were given to do) + HOW WELL (you perform) = ACHIEVEMENT

29) **Get out of the comfort zone**—or the performance won't be interesting to the audience and the performer won't experience any growth.

30) "The mediocre teacher tells. The good teacher explains. The superior teacher demonstrates. The great teacher inspires." ~ William Arthur Ward

TOP TEN LIST FOR GOOD PERFORMERS

#10) Be on time and ready to go. Start stretching and warming up before the class or rehearsal begins. ***Good performers are always ready**! (No injuries, please!)

#9) Prepare for rehearsal with a pencil, notebook, music cued, hair off face, correct dancewear, jewelry off, no gum or candy, proper shoes on—for every rehearsal and performance. ***Good performers are always prepared!** (No excuses!)

#8) Make music when you are supposed to, otherwise, keep the feet quiet. As you walk, walk like a dancer—without a sound. ***Good performers are always respectful!** (Respect the teacher and the class!)

#7) Practice outside of class. Don't hold the rest of the class back because you are the weak link. If you need help, ask. Pursue excellence and not mediocrity. ***Good performers are self-motivated.** (That's why we take notes!)

#6) Don't be scared to smile and have fun in class. If it's not fun, it's not worth doing. ***Good performers aren't afraid to enjoy the moment**. (Go for it!)

#5) No cell phones in class. Teach students who to turn off outside distractions in order to relax and concentrate. If a student's cell phone interrupts my class, he/she has to bring homemade treats for the whole class the following rehearsal. ***Good performers are considerate**. (The best performers are selfless!)

#4) Go with the flow. When we try a new style of dance (hip-hop, lyrical, swing, Latin, novelty, musical comedy, or break dancing), be open-minded. Don't make excuses or shy away from opportunities to grow. ***Good performers are flexible.** (Adapt quickly!)

#3) Listen! Listen with your eyes and ears to the teacher first. Then listen to the music and listen to your self. Use your eyes and ears in proper proportion—two ears, two eyes, and one mouth! ***Good performers pay attention with their eyes and listen with their ears.** (Say only 10% of what you want to say!)

#2) Attend as many different types of live performance as possible: old musicals, Broadway shows, dance recitals, workshops, master classes, recitals, and dance camps. ***Good performers never stop growing**. (Good teachers also keep growing!)

AND FINALLY ...

#1) Don't forget to use "silver boxes" in and out of class. Be thankful for teachers, parents, friends, and God-given talents—for giving you the gift of performance. ***Good performers don't just think of themselves.** (Synergy!!!)

Silver boxes are a concept I've used for over 20 years in my teaching career. My father actually shared the "silver box" story with me. The idea is simple. Let your words be positive and encouraging. When you speak to someone, intend to give a gift (or a silver box) instead of using words that tear down. Rehearsals and the classroom environment are drastically changed when a caring and nurturing attitude prevails in the room. In my experience, students who treat each other with respect learn more, work harder, and enthusiastically anticipate their return. Of course one must be honest with silver boxes and avoid handing out undeserved compliments as students will pick up on this and then the words that were meant to be encouraging will be empty. Wrap your comments like a sandwich. Start with a positive, add the critique, and end with a positive.

Every year, my students take the silver box concept a step further. These photos share actual "silver boxes" that the sophomores decorated and prepared for each freshman with encouraging mementos, photos, and messages on slips of paper. The boxes build camaraderie and allow the group to appreciate and celebrate each member in the ensemble.

BUTLER COMMUNITY COLLEGE HEADLINER POLICIES

1) Attendance at all classes is required. Discuss all possible absences immediately with the director. Unexcused absences may result in dismissal from the ensemble or result in ineligibility for the upcoming year. In the event of a serious illness, contact the director immediately.

2) You must be available for all performances. Do not sign up for additional activities that conflict with performances without getting permission.

3) As this is a performing group, you must be willing to perform whenever needed.

4) Hair must be Headliner standard. Hair that has been colored an unusual color or a different cut (other than what you auditioned with) will not be allowed onstage. If you choose to cut or color your hair, you disqualify yourself from solos or membership from the group. Hair must be out of your face for class. No hats allowed in class.

5) Extreme ear piercings and facial piercings will not be allowed onstage. Belly rings must be removed if they show through costumes. All tattoos must be covered with makeup. No studs—not even clear ones—will be allowed onstage.

6) A healthy weight must be maintained. Members must be able to carry risers, heavy equipment, and instruments up and down stairs. Performers must be able to perform a 2½-hour show at the annual Butler Showchoir Camp in July.

7) You are a role model to all the students and faculty at Butler. We expect you to maintain a high moral standard and act like a professional at all times. There are ears and eyes on you at all times (especially on Facebook). What you do on your time is your choice, but when you are at Butler, or representing Butler, good behavior must be at the highest level.

8) At the discretion of the director, unexcused absences will result in the following: dismissal from Headliners, ineligibility for the next season, and/or loss of a performing part. More than two unexcused absences will result in a student/teacher/dean conference.

9) All in-house workshops are required. You will be expected to attend workshops as stated by the director.

10) If you wish to teach at another school, health center, or dance studio, or post videos on the Internet, you must discuss with the director and obtain permission. You are representing the school and the ensemble as long as you are in the music program, and the material is copyrighted by the director and the publishers.

11) After each and every show, cleanup is REQUIRED for all Headliners. Those who don't circle or help strike may be benched for upcoming performances. Students are auditioning at all times.

12) If unable to uphold all vocal music obligations, the student will be ineligible for the following season.

13) Student drivers will uphold the rules of the college. Student drivers will watch a mandatory video shown by the Butler Facilities Department and these students will be subject to drug tests at any given time.

14) Students must maintain the required GPA and pass 12 hours each semester. Students must not be involved in any episode off campus or in the dorms that reflects poorly and brings bad PR to the vocal music department.

15) Failure to follow and uphold these policies will result in dismissal from the ensemble. All rules and policies are at the discretion of the director.

Continuing the Tradition of Shawnee Press Excellence

Copyright © 2011 by HAL LEONARD CORPORATION
International Copyright Secured   All Rights Reserved
This page may be reproduced.

TOUR/JOURNEY RULES (BONUS!)

1) The only discussion regarding other show choirs, costumes, etc. that will be permitted will be of a positive nature. Negative comments are considered "bus talk."

2) Be positive at all times. Do not air dirty laundry or any comments about any person or ensemble activity at any time. Any Facebook entries will be viewed by faculty members. Think before you post!

3) Promote the school's Fine Arts program. You are representing yourself, the department, the college, and the director at all times.

4) Remember posture and presentation. You must look and act professional at all times.

5) Say only 10 percent of what you are thinking. Being confined on a bus will guarantee lots of stories. Be considerate. Facebook even less. Once something is posted on the web, it will be there eternally and can never be removed.

6) Enjoy the company and get to know other members in the group. If cell phones become a problem, they will be prohibited for certain amounts of time. This is the time to make new connections.

7) Be focused the minute you get off the bus. Time is valuable. One hour sounds like a lot of time to dress and set risers and sound, but there is never enough time. We must be a team at all times!

8) Don't burst into song unless approved by director. Not everyone appreciates spontaneous music.

9) Use good table manners. When going through the buffet line, take a single slice of pizza or a cookie and come back for seconds after everyone has been served. Each gentleman escorts his partner, allowing the lady to go first. Put napkins in laps, keep elbows off table, use utensils instead of hands, put utensils down between bites, don't talk with mouth full, and don't clink glasses. Please enjoy good and edifying dinner conversation. Pretend your mama, grandma, or director and her impressionable children are seated next to you.

10) Be sure an area is cleaner when departing than upon arrival. Don't bring in trash. Other schools may have strict eating and drinking rules. We are guests.

11) Do not place drinks on or near instruments, props, and costumes. Protect all musical equipment.

12) $X = X$. If you are fun to be around and excited about the day and encouraging to all the groups,you will have a great day. The other students will love you onstage and off.

13) No public display of affection (PDA) at any time. The general public should not be aware there are any couples in the group—ever.

14) Thank the bus driver(s) and be sure they are included at mealtime and in conversations. Say thank you to everyone!

15) All tours and performances are fun and educational. Bring back lots of ideas and make great memories. You never know when a talent scout around, or your future boss. Be amazing— onstage and off!

Continuing the Tradition of Shawnee Press Excellence

Copyright © 2011 by HAL LEONARD CORPORATION
International Copyright Secured   All Rights Reserved
This page may be reproduced.

THINGS I'VE LEARNED OVER THE YEARS AND WISH I HAD LEARNED IN SCHOOL!

- Employers like to hire people who are diverse, well-spoken, self-motivated, free-thinking, disciplined, respectful, and respected.

- You will lose your voice as a first-year teacher within the first month of teaching. Learn tricks like raising your hand, clapping patterns, and turning off the lights to get students' attention. Better yet, speak softly so they must listen! What a concept — using dynamics in a music classroom is genius.

- Never be satisfied with your own artistic ability. Someone else will practice harder, study more, and go further. If you want to be great, you must continue to work for it!

- Be ready to play and/or sing these songs in any key at any time:
  - "Happy Birthday"
  - "National Anthem"
  - "Doxology"
  - "Copacabana" (OK — I lied about this one — but it should be required...)

- Females: Get used to people asking if you are "Goth." You will wear lots of black dresses in your lifetime whether it be to conduct, perform, play in the pit, dance in class, or just to dress up in the evening.

- Males in the performing arts: Ignore stupid comments from those on the outside who don't understand what you do. Don't pick a fight or apologize, but be the best at what you do. Let them see for themselves. Sorry, parents — you might also be on that list.

- You will be expected to be an expert on anything having to do with the Arts.

- You may be the big fish in a small pond now, but be prepared for that to change. The arts world is flooded with talented individuals and getting to the top takes perseverance, passion, and a lot of hard work.

- Work on your piano proficiency skills. You must pass basic piano proficiency to get your music-related degree. As a director, you must be able to play the piano to survive in a classroom or in front of any type of music ensemble.

- Prepare to be poor for a while — it takes years to get a regular job in many arts industries. Often, even a great job won't make you wealthy but it can make you happy, healthy, and satisfied.

- You will be asked to share your talents often (even if visiting a church for the first time) and you will receive many requests by music directors to "help out."

- You will have a hard time attending any type of music/dance/theatre performance and just enjoying it. Learn to quit taking notes.

- Use the "day after" approach. When a friend/spouse/sibling asks how he/she did in a performance, you may want to critique, but trust me, wait for at least 24 hours. If the evaluation is important, you'll remember the next day. And if it wasn't, just forget it.

- If you are really good, you don't have to tell that to people.
  ("Big hat, no cattle" ~ Nancy Wesche)

- The secretaries, janitors, and security guards rule the world. Be nice to everyone!

- Connections in this world are important. Not all performers need degrees – it depends on what you want to do.

- All top CEOs have three things in common – involvement in the arts is oftentimes one of them.

- Early morning college theory classes – are they a stepping stone or stumbling block? If you want to be involved in music you are going to have to set your "opportunity clock" (alarm clock) and get to class on time. It is up to you. In the Arts, you must be willing to make sacrifices.

- "What is it that you like doing? If you don't like it, get out of it, because you'll be lousy at it."
  ~Lee Iacocca

- You are part of a great community. Don't be afraid to ask for help when needed.

AUTHOR'S BIO

VALERIE LIPPOLDT MACK

Valerie Lippoldt Mack, music chair and dance instructor at Butler Community College in El Dorado, Kansas, has gained experience and recognition as a music educator and professional choreographer throughout the United States. Her choreography has been featured at Carnegie Hall, Disney World, national ACDA conventions and MENC workshops, the Miss America competition, and various national show choir competitions and festivals around the country. A noted clinician, adjudicator, and director, she has presented and adjudicated more than eight hundred workshops and festivals. She and her husband, Tom, direct the annual Butler Showchoir Showcase each summer in El Dorado, Kansas. Valerie received a Bachelor of Arts from Bethany College and a Bachelor of Music Education and a Masters of Music Education from Wichita State University.

At Butler Community College, Valerie directs the 120-voice Butler Concert Choir, the Butler Headliners Showchoir, and the Smorgaschords Barbershop Quartet, and teaches tap dance, choreography, and private voice. In 2010, the Butler Headliners were one of four finalists in NBC's *TODAY*'s Show Choir Showdown and performed for more than 8.5 million viewers. The Butler Headliners have also done local commercial work and are in constant demand to perform for various state, regional, and national conventions and conferences.

The Smorgaschords barbershop quartet has continuously placed in the International Collegiate Barbershop Competition. Valerie was honored at the 2011 Central States regional barbershop competition, where twenty years of past Butler Smorgaschord barbershop quartets came together to pay tribute to her teaching. She was named a Butler Master Teacher, has won the Golden Apple Teaching Award, has delivered commencement addresses, and is in demand as a motivational speaker for numerous events.

In her spare time, Valerie teaches at the Kansas Dance Academy, directs the Risen Savior Lutheran Church Choir, sings and plays keyboard for the praise team, is on the board of directors for Music Theatre of Wichita, does regional commercial and TV work, is a talent coach for the Miss America program, and is involved with family activities.

Valerie and her husband Tom reside in Wichita with their two children, Stevie and Zane.

Val's top-selling books, *IceBreakers: 60 Fun Activities That Will Build a Better Choir* and *IceBreakers 2: 64 More Games and Fun Activities*, both from Shawnee Press, include favorite team-building activities and fun games as well as encourage students to be positive, focus-minded musicians. Valerie joined Todd Schreiber to co-author *Olympic Games for the Music Classroom*, also published by Shawnee Press. Valerie is also a contributor to various Alfred teacher resource books. *Putting the SHOW in CHOIR!* is one of her newest and most favorite projects.

THE BUTLER COMMUNITY COLLEGE HEADLINERS

EL DORADO, KANSAS

VALERIE LIPPOLDT MACK,
DIRECTOR AND CHOREOGRAPHER

The Butler Community College Headliners from El Dorado, Kansas, under the direction of Valerie Lippoldt Mack, are known nationally for their excellence in the show choir field. Created in 1981, the Butler Headliners provide vital and timeless public relations for the college. Members earn full vocal scholarships with their participation in the Headliners and the 100-voice Butler Concert Choir. The musicians perform four home concerts each year, open the Butler Showchoir Showcase each July and perform in multiple performances in the extended community.

The Butler Headliners were selected as one of the top four finalists in *TODAY*'s Show Choir Countdown, performing on *The Today Show* with Kathie Lee and Hoda for millions of viewers in 2010. The ensemble received many positive comments from show choir enthusiasts worldwide.

The group has filmed and produced commercials for local businesses. Besides performing, the Butler Headliners provide valuable service to the community each year, working with Big Brothers Big Sisters, the United Way, Circle of Friends, and numerous other school, church, and community organizations. Ten years ago the Headliners began a show choir experience for younger children called Kids Showchoir Spectacular, an event that introduces elementary-school children to the joys of singing and dancing.

The Butler Headliners tour each spring and have received regional and national recognition. The Headliners have performed at numerous state, regional, and national ACDA and MENC conventions. The Headliners have been honored with the prestigious Fame Award as well as hosting many Fame show choir competitions. The 40-member group is accompanied by a seven-member instrumental combo led by Joel Knudsen, piano instructor at Butler Community College.

The Headliners are an energetic, exciting young group with a true passion for performing. Each year, the singers look forward to sharing their passion as performers and thank you for your support! Best wishes to each and every one of you in all future endeavors—onstage and off!

Work like you don't need the money.

Love like you've never been hurt.

Dance like nobody's looking.

GO AND MAKE A DIFFERENCE!

Thank you to all who provided photos including Michelle McClendon, Martin Cram, and Matt Udland!

NOTES

NOTES

NOTES

NOTES

NOTES